Soulful Aging

This book seeks to map out the parameters and boundaries of soulful aging and explores philosophical and theological perspectives on the way we grow older. It extends work in the behavioral and social sciences which address the diverse and contested connections of older people's inner voices and social relationships.

Building on qualitative and quantitative research in age studies and gerontology, this volume extends concepts and stories that attest to the joys, tensions, and paradoxes that mount with advancing years. From ten authors versed in writing from multi-disciplinary and inter-professional perspectives with clarity, this book conjoins and challenges behavioral thoughts-and-actions and religious/spiritual spheres of late-life human development previously presented in the context of positive and productive aging as well as healthful, wise, and successful 'Saging'.

Interdisciplinary and insightful, *Soulful Aging* will be a key resource for scholars and researchers of religion, theology, philosophy, psychology, gerontology, and sociology. It was originally published as a special issue of the *Journal of Religion, Spirituality & Aging.*

Author and Retired Professor **W. Andrew Achenbaum** works at the interface of aging, humanities, and policy analysis.

Soulful Aging

Edited by
W. Andrew Achenbaum

Routledge
Taylor & Francis Group
LONDON AND NEW YORK

First published 2024
by Routledge
4 Park Square, Milton Park, Abingdon, Oxon, OX14 4RN

and by Routledge
605 Third Avenue, New York, NY 10158

Routledge is an imprint of the Taylor & Francis Group, an informa business

British Library Cataloguing-in-Publication Data
A catalogue record for this book is available from the British Library

ISBN13: 978-1-032-80294-7 (hbk)
ISBN13: 978-1-032-80297-8 (pbk)
ISBN13: 978-1-003-49631-1 (ebk)

DOI: 10.4324/9781003496311

Typeset in Minion Pro
by codeMantra

Publisher's Note
The publisher accepts responsibility for any inconsistencies that may have arisen during the conversion of this book from journal articles to book chapters, namely the inclusion of journal terminology.

Contents

Citation Information

The chapters in this book were originally published in the *Journal of Religion, Spirituality & Aging*, volume 35, issue 3 (2023). When citing this material, please use the original page numbering for each article, as follows:

A word from the journal editor
A Word from the Editor
James W. Ellor
Journal of Religion, Spirituality & Aging, volume 35, issue 3 (2023), pp. 209

Introduction
A word from the guest editor: A special issue on soulful Aging
W. Andrew Achenbaum
Journal of Religion, Spirituality & Aging, volume 35, issue 3 (2023), pp. 210–211

Chapter 1
Conscious aging, Spiritual aging, and soulful aging: A journey toward the vulnerability of love
W. Andrew Achenbaum
Journal of Religion, Spirituality & Aging, volume 35, issue 3 (2023), pp. 212–221

Chapter 2
I am not aging soulfully
Jon G. Allen
Journal of Religion, Spirituality & Aging, volume 35, issue 3 (2023), pp. 222–226

Chapter 3
Exploring religious/spiritual pathways between practical wisdom and depression: Testing the importance of the divine relationship in later life
Laura Upenieks and Neal M. Krause
Journal of Religion, Spirituality & Aging, volume 35, issue 3 (2023), pp. 227–250

Chapter 4
Finitude and eternity: mental companions of soulful aging?
Frieder R. Lang
Journal of Religion, Spirituality & Aging, volume 35, issue 3 (2023), pp. 251–261

Chapter 5
Slower, deeper, wider: what soulful aging means to me
William L. Randall
Journal of Religion, Spirituality & Aging, volume 35, issue 3 (2023), pp. 262–279

Chapter 6
The Jewish soulful aging of Jacques Élie Derrida
Stephen Katz
Journal of Religion, Spirituality & Aging, volume 35, issue 3 (2023), pp. 280–294

Chapter 7
Soulful ageing- a lifetime cancer journey
Janice Ryan
Journal of Religion, Spirituality & Aging, volume 35, issue 3 (2023), pp. 295–312

Chapter 8
In the twinkling of an eye
Sarah Robinson Flick
Journal of Religion, Spirituality & Aging, volume 35, issue 3 (2023), pp. 313–317

Chapter 9
The poetics of soulful aging
Braveheart Gillani
Journal of Religion, Spirituality & Aging, volume 35, issue 3 (2023), pp. 318–340

Chapter 10
"Take my hand, precious lord and lead me home": Witnessing soulful aging
Karen Skerrett
Journal of Religion, Spirituality & Aging, volume 35, issue 3 (2023), pp. 341–355

Notes on Contributors

W. Andrew Achenbaum, Author and Retired Professor, USA.

Jon G. Allen, Department of Psychiatry and Behavioral Sciences, Baylor College of Medicine, Houston, USA.

James W. Ellor, *Journal of Religion, Spirituality & Aging,* Baylor University, Waco, USA.

Sarah Robinson Flick, Independent Scholar, USA.

Braveheart Gillani, Jack, Joseph and Morton Mandel School of Applied Social Sciences, Case Western Reserve University, Cleveland, USA.

Stephen Katz, Trent University, Peterborough, Canada.

Neal M. Krause, University of Michigan, Ann Arbor, USA.

Frieder R. Lang, Friedrich-Alexander-Universitat Erlangen-Nurnberg, Germany.

William L. Randall, Department of Gerontology, St. Thomas University, Fredericton, Canada.

Janice Ryan, Theology/Philosophy, Dominican University College, Ottawa, Canada.

Karen Skerrett, Psychologist, Consultant, and Author Oak Brook, USA.

Laura Upenieks, Department of Sociology, Baylor University, Waco, USA.

A word from the journal editor

James W. Ellor

Soulful Aging offers an opportunity to explore philosophy/theology's perspectives on the way we grow older. This issue is different from many of those found in this journal for two reasons. First, many of the authors in this issue are themselves older, thus they are speaking with an aging heart of their own. Second, this is philosophy/theology, it is not evidence based. This volume reflects older professionals speaking from the heart. I commend this to your reading.

James W. Ellor
Journal of Religion, Spirituality and Aging, Baylor University
✉ James_Ellor@baylor.edu

Introduction: A word from the guest editor

W. Andrew Achenbaum

I led symposia on spirituality and aging last summer at Houston's Hope and Healing Center and Institute (HHCI), where health professionals deliver mental-health lectures and psycho-social outreach to older persons. Unlike most of the scientific research on late-life wisdom and ripening, I wanted to encourage participants to catch gut feelings that integrated mindfulness, animated heartfelt emotions, and stirred contemplative action in the here and now. Gerontologists, I knew, blazed scientific paths by generating evidence-based reports in the context of positive and productive aging, and/or healthful, successful Saging. As I engaged with HHCI program directors and various audiences of older individuals, however, I discerned that many insights and shadows ascribed to conscious and spiritual aging spiraled into a third component of individuation: with advancing years arose an uncharted, albeit growing and deepening sense of soulful aging along with increasing frailty and intimations of finitude.

I wondered whether mapping out the borders and boundaries of "soulful aging" merited further reflections – but not mine alone. Investigating the topic required collaborative assessments by peers willing to risk expressing conscious, inward reflections. I proposed to Jim Ellor, the general editor of the *Journal of Religion, Spirituality, and Aging*, that we design a special issue on the topic. Three colleagues – Tom Cole, Heike Hartung, and Roberta Maierhofer – helped generate a list of three dozen possible contributors. What follows in this special issue is the first wave of responses.

*The first three essays present my explorations of synergistic links to soulful aging. Menninger psychologist Jon Allen challenges the framework. Laura Upenieks and Neal Krause highlight pertinent findings and refine gems of decades-long survey research into religion, spirituality, and aging.

*Three other colleagues delve into facets of this dynamic tripod. Professor Frieder Lang imagined finitude and eternity to be mental companions of soulful aging. Narrative gerontologist William Randall transformed his nascent ideas into a profoundly scholarly adventure. Sociologist Stephen Katz probed the religious and spiritual impact on Jacques Derrida's paradigmatic hypotheses about grammatology and deconstruction.

*The last four essays recount personal experiences. Caregiver Janice Ryan relates how her steadfast faith healed recurring bouts with cancer. Psychiatrist Sarah Flick, who does spiritual direction along with her husband The Rev. Robert Flick, talks about healing persons who are suffering. Braveheart Gilliani, a doctoral candidate in social work, portrays his authentic identity in terms of the poetics of aging. Therapist Karen Skerrett reconstructs conversations with her late mother, a witness to soulful aging.

We welcome your input. Did some essays pierce your conscious/spiritual/soulful Being and Becoming? Do you wish to suggest other lines of inquiry or additional sentient voices? What reservations do you have about this venture?

W. Andrew Achenbaum

Conscious aging, spiritual aging, and soulful aging: a journey toward the vulnerability of love

W. Andrew Achenbaum

Several decades ago, undergraduates gave me a lithograph inscribed with an aphorism by Hillel the Elder (110 BCE-10 AD), which framed guidelines for individuals seeking to live with integrity until death:

> "If I am not for myself, who will be for me?
>
> And being for myself, what am I?
>
> And if not now, when?"

To me, the Rabbi's three questions metaphorically come alive as a dynamic trio: honesty, candor, and humility. The first animates enough trust to be honest in conscious aging. The second query permits vulnerability to shadows manifest in spiritual aging. The third welcomes in soulful aging a vulnerability in Love.

Neither linear nor epigenetic in a journey with an unknown endpoint, the synergistic interplay of conscious, spiritual, and soulful aging dynamically spirals in circles. Pilgrims like me sense the paradox of God's simultaneously being beyond and near. At every moment the boundless trio tries to integrate self-care, caregiving, and intimacy. We seekers want communion with a life-sustaining Creator, whom in faith and hope we believe is calling us in Love. The diverse convoy moves toward a mystical homecoming – an elusive, ethereal destination – mere mortals cannot imagine or chart, much less attain on our own.

Soulful aging evolves in mindfulness; it taps spiritual wellsprings (and often religious roots). Crises over the life course instigate continuities and changes in developing authentic, holistic identities. Seekers often need to withdraw again and again into themselves; they make time to delve into life reviews, in order to fashion true identities. Awakenings sometimes come about surprisingly, serendipitously in frequency. Transitions vary, too, whether they be aspirational, ecstatic, unnoticed, or frustrating. Transformations can be healthful, irrational, impactful or ineffectual. Dry spells, setbacks, and detours can drive pilgrims to despair as they journey in life.

The unpredictable, synergistic concatenation of conscious, spiritual, and soulful aging encourages seekers to proceed "gentle and humble in heart" (NRSV, Matt 11:29). Through meaning-filled fits and starts during the second half of life, my interior quest began after a mid-life crisis in stepping toward individuation. Being diagnosed as bipolar was humbling but, in retrospect, it was liberating: The greatest enemy of any spiritual journey is self-rejection, since it deafens the voice that calls us "beloved." I regained strength and acknowledged weakness. It helped to join support groups, and read passages from the Psalms, Rumi, Oriental sages, contemporary western philosophers and theologians, and self-help gurus.

My purposive albeit tentative self-reflections then gradually reshaped my professional roles as a teacher, mentor, and historian of aging. I invited on dozens of occasions individuals between ages 22 to 104 to share ruminations about Transcendence (Everything belongs to God), Immanence (God is in everything), and Presence (wherein time dissolves into the here-and-now). Together, we admitted doubts about faith-based traditions, interjecting current qualms and anxieties about uncertainties. We talked frankly, though we did not actually know the width, depth, or endpoint of our searches (Achenbaum, 2021).

Now, Tom Cole, Heike Hartung, and Roberta Maierhofer have agreed to collaborate in co-editing this special issue on "soulful aging." They join two dozen other essayists in revealing personal thoughts, feelings, and experiences about superimposing distinctive paths blazed by conscious, spiritual, and soulful aging. Conveying sentient shards of insight and clusters of unknowing, the authors in this collection make connections and evince serendipitous complementarities, which may pierce and envelop your unique pilgrimages. Taken as a whole, they highlight ironies, contingencies, and lacunae in their own searches, seizing insights and anticipating surprises while thriving and approaching death.

Conscious aging

> "And what is the measure of my days;
>
> Let me know how fleeting my life is." (*NRSV*, Psalm 39:4)

My being semi-retired provides opportunities to relax, volunteer, visit family, and connect with friends. New-found freedoms are inevitably burdened with limitations, stressors, and reduced income, however. Having left professional legacies, self-worth increasingly seems laced with distress, discomfort, constricted options, and loss of authority. "The door between control and freedom is in the mind" (Chittister, 2022).

Conscious aging, I am discovering, renews intentional growth through an open-ended ripening of mind and heart. Dualistic thoughts and straitjacketed feelings give way to tolerating dubiety, ambiguity, mistakes, and misjudgments.

> Insight, courage, and endurance . . . [help us] reclaim personal authority from the vaults of history. Then we may know we have truly moved into the second half of life, the part where we get our life back (Hollis, 2018).

Conscious aging drives my desire for promises of hope, but this imposes the difficult task of shedding long-held attachments and self-defeating behaviors.

Pilgrims traveling with me typically wish to wisely assess choices and conflicts – many with irremediable outcomes. Will divesting career-long competitiveness and conceits presage deeper inward reflections? Can accepting limitations and flaws undercut pride, freeing my coveting status, control, and power?

Unforeseen circumstances can threaten conscious aging. My wife spent ten weeks hospitalized as a cancer patient in 2015. Undergoing one intervention and test after another, she feared losing autonomy. "It may not be dying we fear so much, but the diminished self" (Frank, 1995). I suddenly became an untrained, reluctant, and incompetent caregiver, terrified that my newlywed spouse *was* dying (Achenbaum, 2023). I endured physical, mental, and emotional burnout, along with episodes of depression, rage, hopelessness, and stress.

Barbara and I continue to be circumscribed by fragility, blind spots, and ageism. Yet calamities encountered through conscious aging "have a genius of their own" (Mairs, 1993). With empathy I support my wife and practice self-care in attending to physical, mental, emotional losses, and spiritual pains. They accompany our aging individuation, manifest in suffering and mounting frailty.

> How can we offer companionship when we want to keep our own aging self out of the room, and how can we gently touch the vulnerable spots in old people's lives when we have armored our own vulnerable self with fear and blindness? Only when we enter into solidarity with the aging and speak out of common experience, can we help others to discover the freedom of old age (Nouwen, 1979, 2022).

Unlike Jacob, hip-wrenched wrestling God in Peniel (NRSV Genesis 32:35; Yungblut, 1990), I rarely hallow diminishments as I limp toward the unknown. If ancient prophets and modern-day change agents learned how to walk toward freedom despite their unsteady gaits, so can I and fellow travelers.

Dealing with Hillel's first question empowers me to reflect on polar tensions expressed by another guide to conscious aging:

> A human being is part of a whole, called by us 'universe,' a part limited in time and space. He experiences himself, his thoughts and feelings, as something separate from the rest—a kind of optical delusion of consciousness. This delusion is a kind of prison for us, restricting us to our personal desires and affections for a few persons nearest to us. Our task must be to free ourselves from this prison by widening our circle of compassion to embrace all living creatures and the whole of nature in its beauty (Einstein, n.d.).

Mindful beings must recognize delusions and catch expectations that imprison egocentric emotions. By reaching out with broad compassion, adds Einstein, we can liberate ourselves to glance at wider perspectives on Creation. Conscious aging on journeys of life blends spiritual and soulful complements in deep longings and creative imaginations, which are shadowed by doubts and fears (Einstein, 1950).

Spiritual aging

"You have made my days a few handbreaths
And my lifetime is as nothing in your sight.
Surely everyone stands as a mere breath" (NRSV, Psalm 39:5)

Spiritual aging infuses and enthuses further mindfulness; it recasts awareness of strengths and weaknesses, particularly when seekers like me feel disillusioned and marooned in arid places. Narrating success stories and obsessing about disappointments does little to promote self-care; they neither hide nor extinguish jealous resentments of colleagues or self-deflating comparisons with others.

To cultivate conscious aging and to ripen in spiritual maturity requires acute listening to inner voices in order to re-member laughs and regrets possibly forgotten, suppressed or masked. Having decided to withdraw from the public square and to stay out of domestic feuds, my keenness to read and write about late-life spirituality life creates the "art" of old age in a meditative, iterative process (Delbanco, 2012). My search is facilitated by probing more deeply inward and recalling my narrative stories slowly. With less to lose, I have opportunities to revisit Hillel's three questions as if I were for the first time:

> "If not for myself, who is for me," should holding on to prideful duty matter more than pursuing immanent freedom? "If only for myself, what am I?" in a transcendent milieu, does humility prompt letting go of possessions and privilege? Does realizing "If not now, when?" demand seizing moments in old age for fusing meaning-laden resilience out of being wounded?

Ruminating on the heartfelt pithiness, inherent in the Rabbi's three questions, provokes another query thus far unaddressed: How might connecting conscious and spiritual aging facilitate and/or impede soulful trust within a loving Creator?

Sunday-school teachers said that "Jesus loves me [and] little children," while recounting Good News about the Lord's cosmic caring for all humans on earth; Christ's earthy parables took root as tiny mustard seeds, which grew upward to the sky. These elders nonetheless noted in *sotto voce* that some plantings withered in weeds and parched soil. I was too young and naïve to fathom why this Creator of Eternal Everything and Nothingness was a God

Who Am never capricious, arbitrary, despotic, or cruel. I was instructed to kneel.

Decades later I remain perplexed in relating to this Ultimate Reality. Messages in Scripture seem mixed. That "the fear of the Lord [that] is the beginning of knowledge" (NRSV, Proverbs 1:7) appears more often than any other Biblical clause hardly guarantees heaven on earth, especially IF "the Most High also hates sinners and will inflict punishment on the ungodly" (Ecclesiastes 12:6).

Spiritual aging weaves a counter-narrative, which sanctions, perhaps sanctifies, leaps of faith. Yahweh told Father Abraham to "not be afraid" (Genesis 15:1). The motif, which renders fear into awe, is repeated in Hebrew Scripture (Deuteronomy 31:6; Joshua 1:9; Isaiah 41:10, 13) and, beginning with the Annunciation of a teenage virgin Mary, in the New Testament (John 14:27; Hebrews 13:16; 2 Timothy 1:7). Ambiguous contingencies nonetheless persist. Scriptural definitions of "fear" often appear more terrifying than balm of Gilead.

Fear is real. Panic raises adrenaline. Getting too near snakes and nighttime driving scare me, as I opt for fight or flight. I question whether habitual reflexes, longstanding practices, and hard-wired wisdom realistically accommodate unknowns, or empower successful adjustments to calamities. Choices are unsettling – how and when to press on, stand firm, or to move backward?

Consciously inspired journeys toward the Ineffable are exhausting, even humiliating when I am not in control. Yet the timeless gift of spiritual aging lies in pursuing searches filled with grit and blessed with grace. Listening attentively to God awakens the courage to surrender in patience and silence. Seeing both glimmers of sunlight and thick clouds in the process of examining our inner selves sometimes cracks open empathetic hearts darkened with remorse.

The Hindu guru Sri Ramana Maharshi gave his disciples a meditation, which to my mind parallels Einstein's concern with immanent delusions and transcendent intimations embedded in Hillel's question, "Who am I?":

> It is enough that one surrenders oneself. Surrender is to give oneself up to the original cause of one's being. Do not delude yourself by imagining such a source to be some God outside you. One's source is within yourself. Give yourself up to it. That means that you should seek the source and merge in it (Ramana, 2016).

Spiritual aging produces conscious and soulful branches. It invites giving ourselves up in good times and dark woods to the Source of Being. Might God need me, I wonder, as much as I need God? If so, the Creator's visceral call dares us to reach for "the Lord [who] is the strength of my life; of whom then shall I be afraid?" (Psalm 27:1). Transformative quests elucidate individuated possibilities for assuaging fear and mitigating despair. Intentional, spirit-filled aging bolsters the hospitality of hearts open enough to perceive and receive grace-filled, generous Love palpable in soulful aging.

Soulful aging

> "For I am your passing guest,
>
> an alien, like all my forebears.
>
> Turn your gaze away from me,
>
> that I might smile again,
>
> before I depart and am no more." (Psalm 39:12–13)

May I once again invoke Hillel's three questions, in an effort to wrestle with richer recapitulations of fears of rejection, disinheritance, and abandonment that plague my life? Can I muster sufficient strength and wisdom sufficient to try to forge intrapersonal (immanent) and interpersonal (transcendent) relationships in God's here-and-now Love? Or do I cling to my wounds and doubts rather than trust the vulnerability of Love? Can I ever manage to re-present my aging self as a "passing guest," replicating my forebears, as I stumble consciously and spiritually long for a Friendship, not just a glancing gaze, within a boundless, infinite, Ultimate Reality?

I cannot let go of trepidation over losing control, despite having come this far in struggling to be candid about failings. How likely is it that my honest search for God results in suffering chaotic turmoil and naked despair? What if I ascertain that seeking Love culminates not in union with a Transcendent, Immanent Presence but dissolves into dreadful Nothingness? And therein lies the Hope – to live a soulful aging full of uncertainty and faith.

Gerontologist colleagues astutely identify me as "spiritual and religious" (Bengtson & Silverstein 2019), but their survey data cannot fully contextualize or historicize that designation. My soulful aging transpires in a society paradoxically secular and God-besotted. Thanks to the influence wielded by millions of evangelicals in the alt-right, "Americanized updates of the Gospel has finally completed its victory over older Christian institutions and traditions," thanks mainly to the influence of millions of alt-right evangelicals. "The post-Christian label fits the overall trend in American spirituality more than it did a decade ago" (Douthat, 2022). Manifest meanings of being "religious and spiritual" have been undercut and transmogrified during my lifetime.

Religiously, I am an Anglican who savors the freedom to bend and discard denominational articles of faith. I believe that the Word was made flesh in Creation (Genesis 1:1), and Jesus' birth a later incarnation (John 1: 1–3, 14), emanating intimate encounters with an Ultimate Reality millennia before and after my lifetime. This vulnerability in Love also nurtures epiphanies among agnostics, Brahmins, Buddhists, Jews, Muslims, the non-religious, and in the generational traditions and rituals passed down in indigenous cultures.

My late-life spiritual peregrination, in contrast, evolves into a joyful vocation that seeks to center my heart in a mystical Being. Still faltering, I am able to give thanks to an invisible Connector nourishing bonds not yet intertwined in healing. Thus being "religious and spiritual" is fraught with ambivalence (Allen, 2022; Stromberg, 2022). I reaffirm a desire to surrender my soul to a forgiving God – all the while harboring doubts, missing the mark, and clinging to false masks.

I am inclined to turn first to science to grapple with Hillel's three questions. So do many bio-medical-psycho-social researchers, as well as social workers and healthcare professionals, who generate data and report findings. Experts measure, recalibrate, and debate testable, quantifiable age-based patterns of anomalies, multicollinearity, multi-sectional flips, and inter-subjectivity. "In envisioning the way things are, there is no better place to being than with modern science. Equally, there is no worst place to end" (Smith, 1992).

The challenging quest for conscious, spiritual, and soulful aging continually unfolds existentially. An unimaginable homecoming awaits sojourners. I want to anticipate that my separateness and alienation will be transfigured in a mystical capacity for communion. Martin Buber updates and embellishes Rabbi Hillel's aphoristic tripod with a radical *I-and-Thou* formulation:

> What, then, does one experience of You?
>
> Nothing at all. For one does not experience it.
>
> What, then, does one know of the You?
>
> Only everything. For one no longer knows particulars (Buber, 1923).

Conscious, spiritual, and soulful aging intimately strives to quench my thirst for deeper immanent knowing and transcendent bonding, each and every day. Nothing and Everything may yet succor pain and angst. I pray that living into death unshackles my soul from toxic ambition and arbitrary mandates. Someday, somehow, I shall come to flourish, enveloped in God's healing Love.

Living into dying and death

"Lord, let me know my end" (Psalm 39:4)

Conscious, spiritual, and soulful aging mystically penetrates living and punctuates death. Cognitive decline and physical insults will undoubtedly afflict advanced age, yet "Love is as strong as death, passion as fierce as the grave" (Song of Songs, 8:6). There are novel, transformative opportunities while aging in later life.

This ongoing search, no matter how vital and steadfast, exacts a stiff price. Seekers sooner or later venture towards a sacred canopy with heights not of their making and dimensions not to their liking. Juxtaposing hope and disbelief in tension is sublimely tragic. "Tragedy teaches that viable hope can only arise by first accepting all that is hopeless, and a mature appreciation of tragedy depends on that paradoxical recognition" (Frank, 2022, p. 123). In death, all humans surely let go of constructs freighted in delusions. Sojourners can repent cruel thoughts and misdeeds that once seemed self-satisfying and deemed justifiable.

The Hebrew word for "repentance," teshuva, also means "return." Returning to Hillel's aphorisms once again remains excruciatingly provisional, full of imponderables. Yet heading to the home front, I no longer feel obliged to honor the parameters set in those questions centuries long ago. Where, I wonder, is God's role in all this? "No one can fathom what God has done from beginning to end" (Ecclesiastes 3:12). Will digging deeper reveal more hidden pieces of the sacred whole? Perhaps not: Assessing strengths and shortcomings matter less, ironically, because I shall remain blind – actually oblivious – to Love's potent gifts.

> "If I am not myself, who will be for me?" Does this question expose my grandiosity? Do I take too much pride in a fruitful career as an historian of aging that aligned scientific findings, humanistic perspectives, and policy debates? And what those fruitful collaborations with Tom Cole, Rick Moody, Carroll Estes, Stephen Katz, among others, in deploying critical gerontology as a lens on older people's images and perspectives? How often did I disguise smug superiority whenever scientists and practitioners disrespected our audacious research agenda? Why do I resist giving away self-deprecating liminality (honed at GSA) for myopic, faceless marginality? Disillusionment jostles with "the destruction of fantasies, in the night of the spirit that explains why it is, paradoxically, a part of what theologians have called the 'illuminative way'" (Williams, 1979).

Alone but not disengaged in semi-retirement, can I bear fluctuating between pain and joys, ever more eschewing conventions and rules that no longer feed my soul? Can I finally surrender re-presentations of self-seriousness, pomposity, and grandiloquence? Can I commit to desiring communion with a Soulmate whose Third Eye gazes at incompatibilities of my heart, mind, and soul?

"If I am only for myself, what am I?" Does Hillel's question lay bare my narcissism? Why do I insist on praise after giving toasts at students' weddings by vocalizing Theodore Roethke's cherished poetic line "Love is not love until love is vulnerable?" Do a midlife breakdown and wrenching divorce validate refining, accepting, and celebrating conscious, spiritual, and soulful as exculpatory dispensations? Or is it one of life's sorrows to ascertain that Love respects boundaries, however temptingly permeable they may seem to transgress.

Late-life pathways are littered with hurdles and humiliations, which may initiate moments of forgiving and forgiveness. I remain suspended as a scarred seeker not a powerful god, brandished in pain and despair, burnished in hope and prayer. "Life, if we are honest about it, is made up of many failings and fallings, amidst all of our hopeful growing and achieving" (Rohr, 2011).

> "And if not now, when?" All lives are fragile and transitory. We all risk chronic illnesses and spiritual anguish before returning to dust. One wise surgeon, in terrible pain from prostate cancer, soberly dissected his premonitions before passing: "Like most people, I will probably suffer with the physical and emotional distress that accompany many mortal illnesses, [exacerbated] by the further agony of indecision" (Nuland, 1994). There is more to add: Gyrating in contingent byways and inadvertent detours, "we move from gross, materially bound dimensions ... into more subtle, luminous dimensions of awareness" (Singh, 1998).

We are bound to stumble in the proximity of finitude. Nevertheless, moving toward a soulful Center, tentatively attuned to conscious and spiritual aging, reveals how "we are not human beings having a spiritual experience. We are spiritual beings having a human experience" (Teilhard de Chardin, n.d.). Sojourners inch on paths for the long haul, soulfully surrendering in an ongoing traction between forbearance for shortcomings and honest acceptance of a human condition that is short-lived. Does not this recapitulation expose important boundary issues? Are we not following in less-traveled pathways that sages once traversed, as they marched toward freedom beyond their grasp? Will not lifelong scars and late-life wounds prey on shame and shadows in the "forever unfinished lifework of our species" (Berry, 1987)?

Humility in the vulnerability of Love invites silent, active waiting – in order to be radically present to what may prove to be the pivotal moment. To "be still and know that I am God" (Psalm 46:11) putatively culminates in a homecoming that is mysterious and inexpressible, albeit accessible and intimate.in which I shall stand firm in faith. Once in communion with a welcoming Creator, will I continue to bear pain and suffering? Or as soulful aging beckons us to journey further into the heart of God, will I be joyfully surprised? Approaching finitude holds forth a promise that probably shall never completely be inwardly digested: Conscious, spiritual, and soulful aging maps and encompasses a journey of living into death, one prefigured and unfolding in Love.

Disclosure statement

No potential conflict of interest was reported by the author.

References

Achenbaum, W. A. (2021). Combining spiritual aging and geropsychological development: Easier said than done. *GeroPsych, 34*, 101–107. https://doi.org/10.1024/1662-9647/a000269
Achenbaum, W. A. (2023). Preparing spiritual caregivers. In J. Levison & R. Fine (Eds.), *The pursuit of life* (pp. 209–219). Penn State University Press.
Allen, J. (2022). Personal communication.
Bengtson, V. L., & Silverstein, M. (Eds.). (2019). *New directions in aging, religion, and spirituality*. Taylor and Francis.
Berry, W. (1987). *Home economics*. North Point.
Buber, M. (1923 [1970]). *I and Thou*. (W. Kaufmann, Ed.). Scribner's.
Chittister, J. (2022). The door between freedom and control. Vision and viewpoint newsletter.
Delbanco, N. (2012). *Lastingness*. Grand Central Publishing.
Douthat, R. (2022). The Americanization of religion, The *New York Times*.
Einstein, A. (1950). In A. Calaprice (Ed.), *The new quotable Einstein* (p. 206). Princeton University Press.
Einstein, A. (n.d. November 9). *Words to live by*. In E. Easwaran (Eds.). Nilgiri Press.
Frank, A. W. (1995). *The wounded storyteller*. University of Chicago Press.
Frank, A. W. (2022). *King Lear*. Oxford University Press.
Hollis, J. (2018). *Living an examined life*. Sounds True.
Mairs, N. (1993). *Ordinary time*. Beacon Press.
Nouwen, H. J. M. (1979). *The wounded healer*. Doubleday.
Nouwen, H. J. M. (2022). Daily meditation: To care. October 17.
NRSV [New Revised Standard Version]. (1991). *The new Oxford annotated Bible*, B. M. Metzger & R. E. Murphy (Eds.). Oxford University Press.
Nuland, S. B. (1994). *How we die*. Alfred A. Knopf.
Ramana, M. (2016). *Who am I?* (24th ed.). Sri Ramanasramam.
Rohr, R. (2011). *Falling upward*. Jossey-Bass.
Singh, K. D. (1998). *The grace in dying*. HarperOne.
Smith, H. (1992). *Forgotten truth*. HarperOne.
Stromberg, D. (2022). The eternal hope of the Wandering Jew. www.hedgehogreview.com
Teilhard de Chardin, P. (n.d.). Jesuit resource. https://www.xavier.edu
Williams, R. (1979). *The wound of knowledge*. The Cowley Press.
Yungblut, J. (1990). *Hallowing our diminishments*. Pendle Hill Publications.

I am not aging soulfully

Jon G. Allen

ABSTRACT
The author protests lofty criteria for soulful aging, basing his argument on the centrality of hope, defined as maintaining the balance between presumption and despair. Lofty criteria are presumptuous and a sense of failure to meet them can promote despair. Hope is predicated on reasonable expectations, and challenges inherent in aging call for discerning expectations. One might hope for a "good-enough" life of aging, a criterion that provides ample latitude.

After many conversations about aging and sundry other matters, I received a generous invitation from my friend, Andy Achenbaum, to prepare an article on soulful aging. Per the invitation, soulful aging includes: "Deep immanent knowing within ourselves and transcendent bonding with others in each and every present moment. Emptying our self-centered impulses as we transform ourselves into attentive, empathetic listeners in meaning-laden conversations and relationships. Embracing humility, silence, compassion, respect, and patience." I protest! I'm not doing all this. I do some of it – occasionally. Unable to vault this high bar, I'll just duck under it.

When I read these lofty criteria, I immediately thought about hope, which undergirds this essay insofar as hope figures into soulful aging. I am a clinical psychologist and psychotherapist. I spent many years writing about hope and teaching patients about hope. After retiring from clinical practice, I was invited by my social work colleague, Noblet Davidson, to lead the discussion on hope in her patient-education series on coping with trauma. In these sessions, Noblet started the meetings by asking the patients how they felt about coming to a session devoted to the topic of hope. To my delight, one day a patient responded that she dreaded the session, anticipating that it would be "a bunch of bullshit." In another such meeting, a patient declared that her first thought was, "Oh shit!" These patients anticipated that I would present them with something akin to pie in the sky. When I read the invitation to write about soulful aging, I had a similar feeling of aversion. Yet I had a blueprint for protest.

I was well prepared for patients' expectation of unrealistic aspirations in a talk about hope. Many years ago, I routinely led patient-education groups about depression. I discovered quickly that, if I started by merely enumerating all the things one must do to recover from depression, the patients protested or tuned me out. They felt I knew nothing about the experience of depression or the challenges in recovering from it. Hearing their protests, I came up with the idea of the *Catch-22s* of depression: All the things you need to do to recover from depression are made difficult by the symptoms of depression. Examples abound: Sleep well; insomnia. Eat healthy; lack of appetite or excess appetite. Exercise; lack of energy. Spend time with people; social isolation. Think realistically; negative thinking and rumination. Engage in enjoyable activities; lack of capacity for pleasure – no cerebral joy juice, as psychologist Paul Meehl (1975) presciently put it decades ago. Lastly, the depressed person needs to be hopeful, but hopelessness beckons or prevails. After extensive dialogue with patients in educational groups, I wrote a book on depression with the subtitle, "From Catch-22 to hope" (Allen, 2006). Accordingly, when I started with the Catch-22s of depression, patients thought I might understand what they were going through, and they listened. Keen to avoid abetting hopelessness, I added that it is not impossible to recover from depression (most people do), but recovery is typically slow and difficult. In one group, a young man responded: "I can tell you doc, it's impossible *without help*." Well said; I'll come back to his point.

With this background of stressing obstacles to thriving, I welcomed the expectation of "bullshit" about hope and thanked the patients for voicing their misgivings. I quickly reassured them that I was not going to talk about the wonders of hope with a cheerleading attitude but rather would focus on the enormous challenges of developing and maintaining hope. I proposed that we need hope when we are facing a *plight*—often enough, a realistically dire situation wherein a hoped-for outcome seems highly unlikely (Allen, 2022). Cheerleading is demoralizing. As my mentor at The Menninger Clinic, Paul Pruyser (1987), advocated, we should not confuse hoping with wishing; rather than wishful thinking, hope must be grounded in facing reality. Following Karl Menninger (1987)—and St. Thomas Aquinas, as I learned belatedly (Kinghorn, 2013) – I characterized hope as requiring that we tolerate the ambiguous and uncertain territory between despair and presumption, both of which entail too much certainty (i.e., nothing will get better or all will be well). I emphasized that fear and doubt are companions of hope, not antidotes. Provocatively, I view hope as a problem, not a solution. I was pleased when some patients remarked, at the end of the session, that I had made hope more accessible – reasonable and realistic.

The patients were expecting presumption on my part: "Just get up off your butt and do something productive or enjoyable." With my colleague, Dick Munich, I wrote a blog post, "The J- word" (Allen & Munich, 2015). *Just*. Just say "No!" to depression. Just say No to psychiatric disorders. Just change your brain chemistry while you're at it. *Just age soulfully.* I'm no fan of despair, although I am sympathetic with the (ideally, temporary) respite that giving up can afford. I commend the saying, "When faced with the impossible, give up." I also say that giving up is an under-rated strategy. The problem: judging when the challenge is impossible to meet, such as giving up on a relationship. Patients also fear hope as it portends disillusionment; their fear is based on ample experience with hopes dashed. But hope opens the door to imagining possibilities and, most crucially, hope motivates taking action that makes positive outcomes more likely. In sum, despair gets you nowhere and presumption sets you up for dejection; hope keeps you going.

Accordingly, I am responding to the invitation to write about soulful aging with the potential pitfalls in mind. We might also think of the *Catch-22s of soulful aging*. Ironically, the catch to being soulful is *aging*, for example, insofar as aging entails serious medical conditions, impaired functioning, diminished autonomy in restrictive living situations, innumerable potential losses, financial struggles, and impending death. Undoubtedly, I'm leaving a lot out of this list; you can fill in the blanks. At worst, aging can be conducive to feelings of helplessness and hopelessness. Recall the young man's response to my remark that it is difficult to recover from depression without help. Accordingly, we might propose that it can be impossible for many persons to age soulfully without help. As the present concern with soulful aging rightly implies, spirituality and religion provide an obvious resource. Yet, to belabor my concern with pitfalls, this resource comes with its own Catch-22s, including *spiritual struggles*, for example, conflicts with God, doubts about religious beliefs, friction with family members or institutions, moral quandaries, and a potentially elusive quest for ultimate meaning. Such spiritual struggles are associated with elevated morbidity and mortality (Pargament & Exline, 2022).

Should I hope that I will age soulfully? No. The editors' description sounds patently unrealistic to me. Heavenly. Presumptuous. As I was thinking about writing this tendentious essay, I happened upon a book that validated my attitude, written by a Massachusetts Institute of Technology philosopher, Kieran Setiya (2022), entitled *Life is Hard*. Starting with a brisk review of ancient philosophy, Setiya highlights the traditional assumption that "philosophical reflection on how to live should make our own lives better." While accepting that vision, he continues: "But the aspiration to live well has frequently embraced a more quixotic goal: the best or ideal life" (p. 3), as exemplified in the editors' criteria. As an alternative to "the life you should want to live, if you could live any life at all," Setiya advocates aiming for "the realistic range of good-enough lives." In sum, "To live well in the sense that animates this book is to cope with the ways in which life is hard while finding enough in one's life worth wanting. Philosophy cannot promise happiness or an ideal life, but it can help to lift the weight of human suffering" (p. 8).

Accordingly, Setiya's book is about topics pertinent to the whole of life, all of which are especially relevant to suffering while aging: infirmity, loneliness, grief, failure, injustice, and absurdity. Aptly, he ends with a chapter on hope.

While not aging soulfully, I am not doing badly and have much for which to be grateful. I suppose that anyone in a position to write an essay for this volume might say the same. In my late 70s, with an ordinary range of medical maladies, my health is fairly good. I am blessed with a marriage of more than a half decade and two fine children. Officially retired, I remain professionally engaged, teaching and writing. I continue a lifelong practice of composing and playing jazz piano with friends. I am physically active. But we live under the threats of climate change that cast a pall over the end of my life, compounded by political deterioration that seems unprecedented in my lifetime. In my ever-shortening run, I live in hope – between presumption and despair. But, with the long run in mind, I find hope hard to sustain when I unsoulfully imagine a profoundly dismal future of life on this planet. I routinely asked patients in education groups on hope to state what – if anything – gave them hope. We wrote the array of responses on a white board. "My faith" was a common reply. But my favorite answer of all time came from a young woman: "I can be surprised!" Brilliant; neither presumption nor despair. Her thought is my fallback into uncertainty, leaving a crack open in the door to hope.

What about religion and spirituality as a resource for me? I have been enriched by many years of participation in the Psychotherapy and Faith Conferences offered by the Institute for Spirituality and Health (Nickell, 2012). Yet I am an aging "none," unchurched but moderately spiritual by my own estimation. I resonate with what philosopher Gabriel Marcel (1950) said about God in his Gifford Lectures, given fifty years after William James's (1994) famous lectures, published as the *Varieties of Religious Experience*. In Marcel's words:

> There is a mass of people who imagine that they believe in God, when in fact they are bowing down to an idol to whom any decent theology whatever would undoubtedly refuse the name of God; and on the other hand there are many others who believe themselves to be atheists because they conceive of God only as an idol to be rejected, and who yet reveal in their acts, which far transcend their professed opinions, a totally inarticulate religious belief. It follows from all this that the answer to a referendum on the question, 'Do you believe in God?' ought to be in the great majority of cases, "I don't know whether I believe in God or not—and I am not even quite sure that I know what 'believing in God' is." Note, carefully, the contrast between these formulae and those of the agnosticism of the last century: 'I don't know whether there is a God or not.' (p. 12)

The Oxford English Dictionary (Brown, 1993) dictionary defines *soulful* as "Full of soul or feeling; of a highly emotional, spiritual, or aesthetic nature; expressing or evoking deep feeling." I'd say I'm somewhat soulful in my quiet way. But reread the editors' characterization of soulful aging: "Deep immanent knowing within ourselves and transcendent bonding with others in each and every present moment. Emptying our self-centered impulses as we transform ourselves into attentive, empathetic listeners in meaning-laden conversations and relationships. Embracing humility, silence, compassion, respect, and patience." Philosopher, Daniel Dennett (2013), wrote a book on tools for thinking. One useful tool is the word, "sorta," to express *degrees* of belief. A very useful concept. Am I aging soulfully? Sorta.

Disclosure statement

No potential conflict of interest was reported by the author(s).

References

Allen, J. G. (2006). *Coping with depression: From catch-22 to hope.* American Psychiatric Publishing.

Allen, J. G. (2022). *Trusting in psychotherapy.* American Psychiatric Publishing.

Allen, J. G., & Munich, R. L. (2015). *The J- Word.* Menninger Clinic, SayNoToStigma.com.

Brown, L. (Ed.). (1993). *The new shorter Oxford English dictionary.* Oxford University Press.

Dennett, D. C. (2013). *Intuition pumps and other tools for thinking.* Norton.

James, W. (1994). *The varieties of religious experience: A study in human nature, being the Gifford lectures on natural religion delivered at Edinburgh in 1901-1902.* The Modern Library.

Kinghorn, W. (2013). "Hope that is seen is no hope at all:" Theological constructions of hope in psychotherapy. *Bulletin of the Menninger Clinic, 77*, 369–394. https://doi.org/10.1521/bumc.2013.77.4.369

Marcel, G. (1950). *The mystery of being (Vol. 1: Reflection and Mystery).* St. Augustine's Press.

Meehl, P. E. (1975). Hedonic capacity: Some conjectures. *Bulletin of the Menninger Clinic, 39*(4), 295–307.

Menninger, K. A. (1987). Hope. *Bulletin of the Menninger Clinic, 51*(5), 447–462.

Nickell, C. G. (2012). *Uniting faith, medicine and healthcare: A 57-year history of the institute for spirituality and health at the Texas medical center.* Institute for Spirituality and Health.

Pargament, K. I., & Exline, J. J. (2022). *Working with spiritual struggles in psychotherapy: From research to practice.* Guilford.

Pruyser, P. W. (1987). Maintaining hope in adversity. *Bulletin of the Menninger Clinic, 51*(5), 463–474.

Setiya, K. (2022). *Life is hard: How philosophy can help us find our way.* Random House.

Exploring religious/spiritual pathways between practical wisdom and depression: testing the importance of the divine relationship in later life

Laura Upenieks and Neal M. Krause

ABSTRACT

The last several decades have witnessed the topic of wisdom gaining momentum in the field of positive psychology. In this study, we focus on the potentially important role of religion/spirituality, specifically beliefs about God, as a mediating mechanism underlying the relationship between practical wisdom and depression among older adults. Drawing on a nationally representative sample of older adults from the 2013 wave of the Religion, Aging, and Health Survey (n = 1,497), our results show that practical wisdom is associated with lower depressive symptoms. We also document that three God-related constructs, God-mediated control, trust in God, and gratitude towards God each partially explained the relationship between wisdom and well-being. Taken together, Christian conceptions of God as a personal, divine being, the ultimate attachment figure who is an unconditional source of love and support for believers, may be a target of older adults who have cultivated practical wisdom.

Introduction

As the North American population ages, research that illuminates pathways to well-being in later life takes on increasing importance. The recent and expanding emphasis on the science of positive psychology has framed this issue with respect to individuals' strengths and self-regulatory behaviors that appear to promote positive development as we age (Glück, 2018; Grossmann et al., 2020). One such factor that is traditionally associated with positive aging is *wisdom*. Research on wisdom is growing rapidly (Baltes, 2004; Staudinger & Glück, 2011), and to date, a fair amount of empirical research has focused on whether wisdom is associated with a number of health-related outcomes, including both positive and negative affect (Etezadi & Pushkar, 2013), life satisfaction (Grossmann et al., 2013; Krause, 2016; Le, 2011), global psychological well-being (Webster et al., 2014), and physical health (Judge et al., 2010). Wisdom has also been found to be related to better subjective well-being among older adults (Ardelt, 2003; Etezadi & Pushkar, 2013; Grossmann et al., 2013), even after controlling for socioeconomic assets (Ardelt, 1997). Scholars have suggested that wisdom provides not only clarity of insight into the world but also tools and coping resources to confront and grow from hardships (Ardelt & Jeste, 2018; Ardelt, 2011). Collectively, this research tends to suggest that wise people enjoy better well-being than individuals who are not wise.

Although scholars have been exploring wisdom for thousands of years, perhaps the most well-known work on the topic was conducted by Crisp (2000). Aristotle firmly grounded his study of wisdom within the domain of virtues and the search for a meaningful and happy life. Aristotle further maintained that the ideal life involved more than acquiring several different virtues: instead, *practical wisdom (phronesis)* is needed to regulate, coordinate, and properly implement virtues in daily life.

Since the time of Aristotle, however, research on wisdom, however, has been plagued with difficulty (Grossmann et al., 2020). Simply defining wisdom has proven to be an arduous task. In fact, Staudinger and Glück (2011) have argued that research on wisdom is a "courageous undertaking" (pg.211). We note at the outset that we make no attempt in the current study is made to resolve long-standing debates as to how wisdom is defined. Instead, we draw upon the definition of wisdom offered by Baltes (2004), who suggested that wisdom is reflected in concern with the important and difficult questions about the conduct and meaning of life that is tempered by an awareness of the limits of our knowledge and the uncertainties of life. Baltes (2004) points out that wise people tend to make better judgments, offer sound and practical advice, and display a unique ability to successfully manage a range of virtues. In this study, therefore, we focus on practical wisdom, which is defined as a " . . . master virtue essential to solving problems of specificity, relevance, and conflict that inevitably arises wherever character strengths must be translated into action in concrete situations" (Schwartz & Sharpe, 2006, pg.377). The Aristotelian network of virtues are orchestrated by practical wisdom, making it worthy of further study.

In our assessment of practical wisdom, we address two issues that surround this important virtue in a broader theoretical context. The first concerns testing whether practical wisdom is associated with mental well-being, gauged in the current study by a measure of depressive symptoms. The second focuses on the potentially important role of religion/spirituality, specifically beliefs about God, as a mediating mechanism underlying the relationship between practical wisdom and well-being. As Lundberg (2010) notes, one of the primary objectives of every major faith tradition in the world is to transmit a number of virtues including humility, compassion, gratitude, and wisdom, to its followers. A key issue that we see to understand is to identify the ways in which wisdom may underlie an important element of religiosity, as defined by one's divine relationship. As we will show, wise older adults tend to have stronger feelings of God-mediated control (that God is a collaborative partner in one's life) and show higher levels of trust in God and gratitude towards God. In what follows, we present a conceptual framework where wisdom promotes a deeper and more meaningful relationship with God, ultimately underlying the robust association between wisdom and well-being that has been empirically documented.

Elaborating a definition of practical wisdom

A number of theories have emerged to describe what wisdom is and how it arises (e.g., the Berlin Wisdom Paradigm; Baltes & Staudinger, 2000). In addition, several scales have been developed to measure wisdom empirically (Ardelt, 2003; Grossmann et al., 2020). However, progress in the study of wisdom has not come without struggle, because wisdom is such an elusive construct; indeed, it is challenging to define and even more difficult to measure well.

The *three-dimensional wisdom model* was created by Monika Ardelt (Ardelt, 1997, 2003) and used to operationalize personal wisdom as an integration of (1) cognitive, (2) reflective, and (3) compassionate dimensions. Within this framework, wisdom is understood as a developmental construct rather than a stable personality trait, which implies that wisdom may increase with age if the motivation exists to engage in psychological growth (Ardelt, 2011; Baltes & Staudinger, 2000). For example, in Erik Erikson's (1982) stage model of psychosocial development, wisdom is the virtue that is gained in later life if all eight developmental life course stages are successfully resolved. Indeed, the *cognitive dimension* of the three-dimensional model of wisdom references the desire to understand deeper truths, particularly about personal and interpersonal aspects of life. This fosters knowledge about the positive and negative aspects of human nature, the limitations of human knowledge and of life's uncertainties and unpredictable nature. To attain this level of understanding, one must engage in self-reflective thinking to perceive phenomena and events from multiple perspective – representing the *reflective dimension* of wisdom. Moving through this process tends to reduce self-centeredness and foster an increased acceptance of human nature and an awareness of the suffering of others, resulting in greater compassion for those in need and generating the motivation to help others in need – this representing the *compassionate (affective) dimension* of wisdom.

As we noted above, we focus on practical wisdom, which contains elements of Ardelt's (1997, 2003) three-dimensional model of wisdom. Practical wisdom helps people resolve problems and challenges that arise by allowing them to translate virtues and character strengths into tangible action (Schwartz & Sharpe, 2006). Picking up on Ardelt's cognitive dimension of wisdom, practical wisdom dovetails with Baltes' (2004) assertion that wisdom is reflected in concern with the important and difficult questions about the meaning of life, which is undergirded by an awareness of the limits of knowledge and uncertainties of life.

Practical wisdom therefore entails the capacity to see what is best (broadly defined) beyond the immediate situation (Zagzebski, 1998). This, in turn, aids in regulating the specific situational virtue in service of this higher goal (e.g., whether to choose compassion or loyalty based on what is good). Practical wisdom is thus comprised of both the motivation to operate at this broader level as well as the ability to effectively execute this action. As Zagzebski (1998) argued, " . . . we ought to consider the virtue of phronesis, or practical wisdom, as a higher-order virtue that governs the entire range of . . . virtues" (pg.229). This means that a practically wise person responds to situations in life by choosing to activate an appropriate virtue in service of the greater good.

Wisdom and well-being: Integrating depressive symptoms

Despite its utility in guiding and directing virtues, practical wisdom may accomplish much more than this and have salubrious benefits for well-being. As we noted earlier, a number of studies indicate that greater wisdom is associated with a range of well-being outcomes, including greater happiness (Bergsma & Ardelt, 2012), greater life satisfaction (Taylor et al., 2011), and a more positive affect (Etezadi & Pushkar, 2013). As one objective of the current study, we contribute to research on practical wisdom and well-being by assessing an outcome that has not been frequently investigated in previous studies: depressive symptoms.

From a theoretical standpoint, wise individuals are generally expected to be happier or more satisfied with their lives. St. Thomas Aquinas agreed with Aristotle that practical wisdom was essential to the human condition (Kristjánsson, 2010). From both an Aristotelian and Thomistic perspective, a virtuous person would have at their disposal a repertoire of virtuous actions to express in appropriate contexts.

The practical implementation of virtues may be especially important for older adults. The latter phases of the life course are accompanied by physical, mental, and social losses (Aldwin & Igarashi, 2015). While adverse life events can undoubtedly happen at all stages of the life course, older adults are more likely to encounter such occurrences as the death of friends and family members, or physical health problems, which tend to adversely impact mental well-being (Clemence et al., 2007; Kraaij et al., 2002). However, wise older adults might have the equanimity and capacity to cope with adversity without letting it affect their mental well-being (Aldwin & Igarashi, 2015; Ardelt & Ferrari, 2014), particularly if they gained wisdom through the process of successfully overcoming previous adversity (Linley, 2003). Wise people might become experts in dealing with the hardships of life, which could explain why wisdom tends to relate to mental well-being, especially when objective life circumstances are not ideal (Ardelt, 2011). As Walsh (2015, pg.285) astutely notes, " . . . wisdom involves expertise in reducing suffering and enhancing well-being both for oneself and others."

The reflective dimension of wisdom seems to be most closely linked to greater mental well-being. Through reflection, people are able to view a challenging situation from multiple angles instead of trying to blame others or circumstances for their misery (Ardelt, 2003). By being aware and mindful of their emotions, wise individuals may be better able to regulate and ultimately overcome negative emotions, such as blame, bitterness, and despair through an acceptance of reality and a forgiveness both of oneself and others (Ardelt and Ferrari, 2014; Ardelt, 2011). Altogether, Monika Ardelt (2019) argued that the ability to maintain a high level of well-being in the face of very negative experiences is a core component of wisdom.

It is clear from the research discussed above that wisdom may be associated with elevated positive affect. But might wisdom also be useful in staving off depression, characterized by feelings of sadness, hopelessness, and a general malaise towards life? Levenson et al., (2005) suggest that the core component of wisdom is self-transcendence: accepting oneself as one is, overcoming the limits of one's ego, existing independent of external sources of self-esteem such as power or fame, and maintaining connection to others and the world at large.

The idea that wise people are deeply at peace with themselves and the world in which they live leads us to expect that practical wisdom will likewise bear a beneficial association with negative affect too. Weststrate and Glück, (2017) over three reasons why wise individuals might be high in well-being: (1) they are effective at coping with life challenges, and can manage difficult situations and regulate negative emotions; (2) because of their experience with hardship, they can appreciate small pleasures and good moments even during challenging times, which should decrease negative affect; and (3) they have learned to live virtuous lives in ways that are meaningful to them, providing them with resources (e.g., supportive relationships) that can support them through challenging times. Taken together, wise people maintain a broad orientation to life that helps them frame the difficulties they encounter. More specifically, they know that troubles will eventually pass. This provides great comfort as well as hope for the future. These are all strong antidotes to the negative fallout from the inevitable trails they encounter.

Empirically, Etezadi and Pushkar (2013) show that the pathway from wisdom to better psychological well-being works through a better coping style (problem-focused coping and positive re-interpretation), a greater sense of meaning in life, and greater perceived control (mastery) over one's environment. We argue in the next section that wisdom may also promote a deeper and more meaningful relationship with God, an important component of religion/spirituality which could lie on the pathway towards greater well-being.

Hypothesis 1: Greater practical wisdom will be associated with fewer depressive symptoms.

Wisdom and god constructs: Pathways to well-being

After conducting a thorough review of the literature, Hood, Hill, and Spilka (2009) argue that wisdom is explicitly described as a virtue in many faith traditions around the world. However, they go on in their review to note that "little or no research" has investigated the relationship between any dimension of religiousness and wisdom (Hood et al., 2009, pg.429). A second purpose of the current study is to address this gap in the literature. We do so by considering constructs related to an individuals' relationship with God. In all Christian religious traditions, God is conceived as a personal being and the source of all goodness and love (Schieman et al., 2005, 2017; Ward, 1994), the 'ultimate friend" and attachment figure who is an unconditional source of support and who is actively engaged in daily human affairs (Kirkpatrick, 2005).

One of the primary functions of religion is to help people live virtuous lives. Every major religious tradition extols the virtues of forgiveness, compassion, and gratitude to God (Lundberg, 2010). Chief among the virtues that are related to religion/spirituality are forgiveness (Davis et al., 2013), feeling grateful to God (Krause, 2012) and helping those who are in need (Krause, 2009). Among older adults, belonging to a religious community was associated with greater practical wisdom (Krause & Hayward, 2014). Wink and Dillon (2013) also found that spirituality at the later stages of the life course (ages 50 and onwards) was associated with greater wisdom in later life.

However, while some studies show that religion relate underlie wisdom, there are other studies that do not support this conclusion. For example, Brezina and van Oudenhoven (2012) did not find any significant relationships between religiosity and wisdom. The more complex interlinkages between the constructs are also indicated by work conducted by Adamovová (2013), who finds that religious orthodoxy is associated with cognitive and reflective dimensions of wisdom, but not with the affective dimension. As Wink and Dillon (2013) suggest, religiosity might be associated with wisdom because it promotes good social judgment and generativity, but on the other hand, religion does not have to lead to insight and introspectiveness, which are key properties of wisdom.

Building on this last point, it is possible that these ambiguities occur because wisdom is the catalyst to religiosity. In other words, wisdom may exist *prior to* the development of religious constructs. Conceivably, it is wise individuals who choose to dedicate their lives to faith and a higher power. In these situations, wise people may be more likely to turn to their faith in times of trouble and hardship, engaging in processes of religious coping in the process (Ai et al., 2007; Jackson & Bergeman, 2011). Indeed, one of the purposes of wisdom is to find deeper meaning in life and human existence (Ardelt & Edwards, 2016; Ardelt, Achenbaum, & Oh, 2013), which can be achieved by turning to one's faith. A key feature of religious life is that it gives ultimate meaning and purpose to one's life through the establishment of an "all-embracing sacred order" (Berger, 1969, pg.51) that allows people to establish meaning when confronted with suffering, misfortune, illness, and death (Ardelt, Ai, & Eichenberger, 2008; Pargament et al., 2005). As we argue below, wisdom may be the precursor to stronger God-mediated control beliefs, a stronger propensity to trust God, as well as greater gratitude to God. These variables, in turn, may be able to explain *why* wise individuals are expected to report fewer depressive symptoms.

God-Mediated Control: As defined by Krause (2005), God-mediated control refers to the belief that God is a collaborative partner with humans in dealing with problems in life. Being wise may prime stronger notions of God-mediated control. One of the hallmarks of wisdom is the realization that one cannot handle the challenges of life, nor the challenges associated with aging, on their own (Ardelt, 2019). Wise individuals may therefore recognize their need to rely on sources of assistance outside of themselves. Believers with stronger beliefs in God-mediated control may have a constant reminder that they are not alone and have a collaborator willing to traverse the difficulties that are faced with them.

People who are wise also know they are not completely in control of everything they encounter in life (Ardelt, 2019). Consequently, they have learned to wait or look for God to intervene. Should this occur, they are likely to place greater faith in the role that God may play in their lives (i.e., they should develop stronger God-mediated control beliefs). But for this to happen, the focal person must be wise enough to look for it and interpret it in the context of God mediated control. In turn, stronger beliefs in God-mediated control are associated with better mental and physical health (Krause, 2005, 2010; Upenieks & Ford-Robertson, 2022). As suggested by Krause (2010), the resources or support that God is capable of providing in times of stress by working together with humans are far greater than the benefits that can be attained from relying on other humans or strictly on oneself. Therefore, to the extent that wisdom among older adults leads them to acknowledge the operative hand of God in their lives, we would expect God-mediated control believes to mediate the relationship between wisdom and depressive symptoms:

Hypothesis 2. The association between practical wisdom and lower depressive symptoms will be mediated by stronger God-mediated control beliefs.

Trust in God: Trust is a primary component of faith, emphasized by most major religious traditions for initiating and maintaining a relationship with God. Trust is necessary for faith because the answers that faith traditions provide must be taken on trust alone. Bancroft summarizes what it entails to have unconditional trust in God: "[t]o believe God is to rely upon, or have unhesitating assistance of, the truth of God's testimony, even though it is unsupported by any evidence; and to rely upon or have unfaltering assurance of the fulfillment of His promises, even though everything seems against fulfillment." The importance of this religious construct cannot be overstated – and yet, it is again likely that wisdom is needed to know how to trust God when faced with difficulties and without tangible proof at hand. Trusting in God involves taking a risk that God will be involved in their lives and come through in a positive way, according to His time and His plan (Pace, 2020). Wisdom is no doubt required as believers wait on God or engage in prayer or other spiritual practices until a person gains a clearer sense of what they can expect from God.

A few studies have revealed that trust in God is associated with favorable well-being, including depression and life satisfaction (Fadardi & Azadi, 2017; Krause, 2015; Rosmarin et al., 2009). Trust in God may help people to manage stressful situations, possibly blunting the pernicious effects of stress and adversity (Pargament et al., 2001). Wise older adults may come to show greater trust in God, again recognizing the limits of human finitude and trusting in God's promise of the afterlife as the end of life nears. We therefore expect:

Hypothesis 3. The association between practical wisdom and lower depressive symptoms will be mediated by stronger trust in God.

Gratitude to God: Our final God-related construct that we propose as a mediator of the wisdom and depression link is gratitude towards God. Gratitude to God is a specific form of gratitude involving, "feelings of thankfulness from receiving a gift from God that may be tangible, emotional, or spiritual in nature" (Krause, 2012, pg.119). Gratitude towards God may be useful to the extent that it reminds individuals of what they have already been blessed with, serving to reduce stress and worry (Upenieks and Ford-Robertson, 2022). A relationship between wisdom and gratitude seems intuitively possible: both wise and grateful individuals tend to be aware of positive outcomes and negative events, recognize that they have limited control over events, and know that it is important to relate to (divine) others. Reflection and integration of negative experiences comprise both wisdom and gratitude

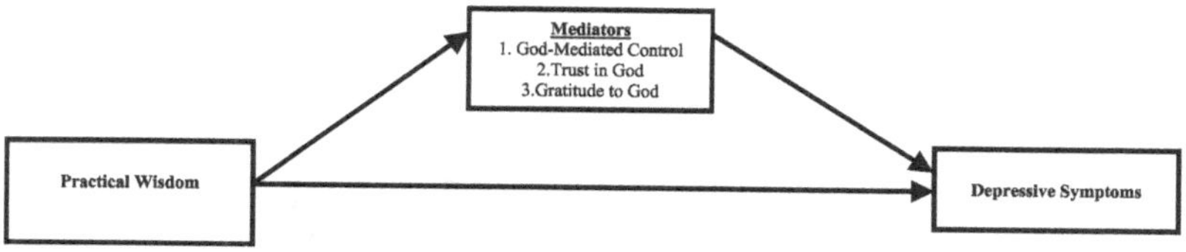

Figure 1. Conceptual model linking practical wisdom and well-being through god-related construct.

(Tennen and Affleck, 2002). Wise individuals also tend to be aware more of others and their connectedness to others and the world at large (Ardelt, 2003; Emmons and Kneezel, 2005) and may appreciate the resources that are available to them, including a relationship with a divine being.

Previous studies have documented a positive relationship between wisdom and gratitude (Konig & Glück, 2013). Although many people may take their lives for granted, wiser individuals tend to be more aware of the fact that one must be grateful for the resource and relationships they possess. Cultivating greater gratitude towards God, the source of all creation in Christian faith traditions, may be conducive to dealing with the demands of life in a wise and self-transcendent way (Levenson et al., 2005). Extant evidence suggests that gratitude to God is associated with lower depressive symptoms (Krause et al., 2014) and greater physical well-being (Krause, Emmons, Ironson, & Hill, 2017; Upenieks & Ford-Robertson, 2022). Here again, to the extent that wisdom allows older adults to express gratitude to God for His divine grace, we would expect this to mediate the association between wisdom and depression:

Hypothesis 4. The association between practical wisdom and lower depressive symptoms will be mediated by greater gratitude towards God.

Figure 1 displays our conceptual framework that we will test in this study. Since we are testing three mediating pathways between wisdom and depression (God-mediated control, trust in God, and gratitude to God), our study design also allows us to compare the relative proportion of our main focal association explained by each mediator, enabling a comparison of the strength of each God-related construct.

Data and methods

Sample

The data for this study come from an ongoing nationwide survey of Whites and African Americans. Altogether, five waves of interviews have been conducted. The study population for the baseline survey was defined as all household residents who self-identified as either Black or White, were noninstitutionalized, English-speaking, and at least 66 years of age. Geographically, the study population was restricted to all eligible persons residing in the coterminous United States (i.e., residents of Alaska and Hawaii were excluded). Finally, the study population was restricted to currently practicing Christians, individuals who were Christian in the past but no longer practice any religion, and people who were not affiliated with any faith at any point in their lifetime.

This study was designed to explore a range of issues involving religion. As a result, individuals who practice a faith other than Christianity were excluded because it would be too difficult to devise a comprehensive battery of religion measures that would be suitable for individuals of all faith. The sampling frame consisted of all eligible persons contained in the beneficiary list maintained by the Centers for Medicare and Medicaid Services (CMS). A five-step process was used to draw the sample from the CMS Files (Krause, 2002).

The baseline survey took place in 2001. The data collection for all waves of interviews was conducted by the Harris Interactive (New York). A total of 1,500 interviews were completed, face-to-face, in the homes of the study participants. African Americans were oversampled so that sufficient statistical power would be available to assess racial cultural differences in religion. The overall response rate for the baseline survey was 62%. Sampling information for Waves 2 to 4 is as follows: Wave 2 (2004), $n = 1024$ (re-interview rate = 80%), Wave 3 (2007), $n = 969$, (re-interview rate = 75%), Wave 4 (2008), $n = 718$ (re-interview rate = 88%).

A fifth wave of interviews as completed in June 2013. However, the sampling strategy for this round of interviews was complex. By the time the Wave 5 interviews were conducted, only 229 study participants were re-interviewed successfully. Many former study participants experienced significant health problems that were associated with their advanced age ($M = 83.2$ years). Moreover, a number of former study participants died ($n = 611$). So, in order to have sufficient statistical power to conduct meaningful analyses, the following two-part sampling strategy was employed. First, we re-interviewed as many of the original study participants as possible ($n = 229$). The re-interview rate for people who had participated in the study previously was 63%. Second, this group was supplemented with a new sample of individuals who had not participated in the study previously ($n = 1306$). In the process of fielding the sample of new study participants, we lowered the age of eligibility from 66 to 50. This was done to make it possible to evaluate issues involving religious involvement to midlife, which is not the focus of the current study. The re-interview rate for prior study participants was 63%. The response rate for people in the new supplementary sample was 45%.

The sample of individuals who had not participated previously in the study was obtained in the following manner. Based on data in the 2010 Census, 50 geographic areas (i.e., Census tracts) were selected to proportionately represent the population aged 50 and above who were either White or African American. All households within each Census tract were enumerated. One eligible person within each household was selected at random to participate in the study. The response rate for the individuals who had not participated in the study previously was 45%. Altogether, a total of 1,535 individuals participated in the Wave 5 interviews. The analyses presented below are based on the Wave 5 data only because this was the first time that questions on wisdom were administered. After eliminating those respondents who had missing data on our study variables, we are left with an analytic sample of $n = 1497$.

Measures

Dependent variable

Depressive Symptoms: Four items that measure a depressed affect were taken from the Center for Epidemiologic Studies Depression Scale (Radloff, 1977). These indicators were as follows: (1) "I felt like I could not shake off the blues, even with the help of my family and friends," (2) "I felt depressed," (3) "I had crying spells," and (4) "I felt sad. Responses were scored where 1 = "Strongly Disagree," 2 = "Disagree," 3 = "Agree," and 4 = "Strongly Agree" and summed across all four items. A higher score on these items denotes a more depressed affect ($\alpha = .85$).

Focal independent variables

Practical Wisdom: Seven items were developed especially for this survey to assess practical wisdom. Based on the procedures described by Krause (2002), the following item development strategy was devised to create these measures. First, 41 open-ended, in-depth interviews were conducted to see what the typical individual thinks about practical wisdom. Following this, the main themes that were extracted from these interviews were used to craft closed-ended items. Once a preliminary set of measures were in place, 40 cognitive interviews were conducted with a new sample of study participants. Cognitive interviews involve presenting respondents with newly developed closed-ended items followed by a series of open-ended probes. The probes were designed to determine if the item is understood in the intended manner and if there are better ways to phrase the question stems.

After this process was complete, the following seven indicators were revised and evaluated with standard pilot testing procedures: (1) "Over the years I've found that wisdom has a lot to do with learning from my mistakes,' (2) "Over the years, I've found that learning when to forgive is an important part of what it takes to be wise," (3) "Over the years I've found that part of being wise involves learning when to help people who are in need," (4) "Over the years, I've found that learning to understand others is an important part of what it takes to be wise," (5) "Over the years, I've learned that part of being wise involves accepting the fact that I will never understand everything in my life," (6) "Over the years, I've learned that part of being wise involves accepting the fact that some things in my life cannot be changed," and (7) "Over the years, I've learned that being wise involves being able to see both sides of a difficult situation and coming to a conclusion that is fair to everyone" (scored where 1 = "strongly disagree," 2 = "disagree," 3 = "agree," and 4 = "strongly agree"). A higher score on the practical wisdom indicators means that a person is wiser, ranging from 14 to 28 ($\alpha = 0.91$).

God-Mediated Control: God-mediated control was positioned as a mediator in our study and was measured by a three-item index. These items were, (1) "I rely on God to help me control my life," (2) "I can succeed with God's help," and (3) "All things are possible when I work together with God." For each item, responses were scored according to the following scheme: 1 = "Strongly disagree," 2 = "Disagree," 3 = "Agree," and 4 = "Strongly agree." Scores were averaged to create a summary measure of beliefs in God-mediated control ($\alpha = 0.94$).

Trust in God: The detailed qualitative procedures of Krause (2002) discussed above were also used to craft measures of trust in God. Following this, the indicators were revised and evaluated with the standard pilot testing procedures. The final five items were, (1) "I trust God completely," (2) "I believe that God will never let me down," (3) "I know that God will ultimately do what is best for me," (4) "I know God will never give me more than I can handle," and (5) "I trust God because He has always been right there for me in the past." The items were scored according to the following scheme: 1 = "strongly disagree," 2 = "disagree," 3 = "agree," and 4 = "strongly agree." Responses were summed and yielded a measure that ranged from 5-20, where higher scores represent greater trust in God ($\alpha = 0.86$).

Gratitude to God: Respondents were asked to respond with their levels of agreement to the following prompts (see Krause, 2006): (1) "I am grateful to God for all he has done for me," (2) "If I were to make a list of all the things God has done for me, it would be a very long list," (3) "As I look back on my life, I feel I have been richly blessed by God," and (4) "I am grateful to God for all he has done for my family members and close friends." Responses were coded on a Likert-type scale where 1 = "Strongly disagree," 2 = "Disagree," 3 = "Agree," and 4 = "Strongly agree." We averaged these four items to form a scale ($\alpha = 0.96$).

Control variables

Several additional covariates were included in all analyses to ensure than any relationship between wisdom and mental well-being is not confounded by other variables commonly known to associate with depressive symptoms and religiosity among older adults. We control for the gender (male = 1) and marital status (married = 1; 0 = otherwise) of the respondent. We also adjust for the number of years of education the respondent had attained over their life course (coded continuously in years), respondent age (measured in years) and race/ethnicity (0 = White, 1= Black).

Additional controls adjust for several religious covariates which could also confound the relationship between wisdom and mental well-being. First, we included a measure of church attendance, gauged by the question, "How often do you attend religious services?" Responses were initially coded into nine categories, but we ultimately coded attendance into a four-category variable, with (1) Never attends, (2) Attends yearly, (3) Attends monthly, and (4) Attends weekly or more. We also adjust for how often a respondent engaged in frequent prayer. This was coded into a four-category variable where (1) Never prays, (2) Prays monthly, (3) Prays weekly, and (4) Prays daily or more. Finally, we include adjustment for religious denomination at Wave 5. This was coded where (1) Protestant, (2) Catholic, and (3) Other Christian.

Plan of analysis

A series of regression models with robust standard errors were used to test our hypotheses. To test the indirect effect (IE) of sense of meaning in life on each of our focal relationships, we employ Sobel- mediation analyses (Hayes, 2013). Finally, listwise deletion was used to handle missing data, yielding a final sample size of $n = 1497$.

We considered a series of four models. Model 1 regressed depression on wisdom, serving as a test of Hypothesis 1. Models 2–4 add in each God-related construct as a mediator, introducing God-mediated control, trust in God, and gratitude towards God in each model. We then conduct a Sobel-Goodman mediation test for the indirect effect of wisdom on depressive symptoms, adjusting for all other study covariates. We then report the indirect effect, the corresponding Z-score and probability value, and the percent of the association between wisdom and depressive symptoms is explained by each God-related construct.

Results

Table 1 displays all descriptive statistics for our study variables. We would note that the average respondent reported 12.62 depressive symptoms (range 4–32, SD = 5.26). In addition, respondents reported fairly high practical wisdom

Table 1. Descriptive statistics, 2013 religion, aging, and health survey ($n = 1497$).

	Mean/%	S.D.	Minimum	Maximum
Dependent Variables				
Depressive Symptoms	6.11	2.72	4	16
Focal Independent Variables				
Practical Wisdom	24.56	3.06	14	28
God-Mediated Control	10.53	1.88	3	12
Trust in God	17.74	3.10	5	20
Gratitude to God	14.45	2.22	4	16
Control Variables				
Education (years)	13.08	2.24	3	20
Age	63.28	11.65	50	102
Married	41.55			
Male	39.35			
Black	35.58			
Religious Affiliation				
Mainline Protestant	40.79			
Catholic	16.58			
Other	42.64			
Religious Attendance				
Never Attends	11.69			
Attends Yearly	25.61			
Attends Monthly	13.20			
Attends Weekly or More	49.51			

Note. Standard deviations are omitted for categorical variables.

scores (mean = 24.56, SD = 3.06). Respondents also reported average God-mediated control beliefs of 10.53 (range 3–12, SD = 1.88), trust in God scores of 17.74 (range = 5–20, SD = 3.10), and gratitude towards God scores of 14.45 (range = 4–16, SD = 2.22).

Multivariable regression results

Main regression results with depressive symptoms as the outcome are shown in Table 2 as unstandardized coefficients. Results for all mediation analyses are presented in Table 3.

Beginning with Model 1 of Table 2, we see that practical wisdom is associated with lower depressive symptoms, net of all study covariates ($b = -0.11$, $p < .05$). This result is consistent with Hypothesis 1 and suggests that those with higher practical wisdom tend to report fewer depressive symptoms.

Models 2–4 introduced each God-related construct sequentially. We focus on what happens to the focal association between wisdom and depressive symptoms, and the association between each God-related construct and depressive symptoms. After each model, we then discuss the results of the Sobel-mediation test testing whether each God-related construct could account for some of the association between wisdom and depressive symptoms.

Model 2 introduced God-mediated control into our analytic model. As shown in Table 2, the association between wisdom and well-being is reduced to non-significance ($b = -0.06$, $p > .05$). On its own. God-mediated control was

Table 2. Wisdom and depression: mediating pathways through god-mediated control, trust in god, and gratitude to god 2013 religion, health, and aging survey ($n = 1497$).

	Model 1	Model 2	Model 3	Model 4
Practical Wisdom	−0.11*	−0.06	0.01	−0.01
	(0.05)	(0.06)	(0.06)	(0.06)
Mediators				
God-Mediated Control		−0.22*		
		(0.10)		
Trust in God			−0.25***	
			(0.06)	
Gratitude to God				−0.34***
				(0.09)
Education (years)	−0.18*	−0.17*	−0.19*	−0.19*
	(0.08)	(0.08)	(0.08)	(0.08)
Age	−0.03	−0.03	−0.03	−0.03
	(0.02)	(0.02)	(0.02)	(0.02)
Married	−1.25***	−1.37***	−1.41***	−1.19**
	(0.35)	(0.35)	(0.36)	(0.35)
Male	−0.58	−0.48	−0.44	−0.68
	(0.35)	(0.35)	(0.36)	(0.36)
Black	−1.09**	−0.81*	−0.71	−0.76*
	(0.36)	(0.36)	(0.37)	(0.37)
Religious Affiliation (ref. = Protestant)				
Catholic	−0.43	−0.44	−0.46	−0.43
	(0.22)	(0.23)	(0.25)	(0.23)
Other Christian	0.25	0.26	0.26	0.26
	(0.14)	(0.15)	(0.15)	(0.15)
Religious Attendance (ref. = Never attends)				
Attends Yearly	−1.29	−1.31	−1.31	−1.30
	(0.76)	(0.79)	(0.75)	(0.74)
Attends Monthly	−1.61**	−1.63**	−1.60**	−1.60**
	(0.58)	(0.60)	(0.57)	(0.58)
Attends Weekly or More	−1.26*	−1.22*	−1.21*	−1.22*
	(0.59)	(0.60)	(0.58)	(0.59)
R^2	0.09	0.10		

Notes. *$p < .05$, **$p < .01$, ***$p < .001$.Unstandardized coefficients and robust standard errors shown in parentheses.

Table 3. Sobel mediation analyses, practical wisdom→god-related constructs→depressive symptoms 2013 religion, health, and aging survey ($n = 1497$).

God-Related Variable	*Z*-score	Indirect Effect	*p*-value	% Mediated
God-Mediated Control	−2.47	−0.04	*	25.75%
Trust in God	−3.85	−0.08	***	54.01%
Gratitude to God	−3.69	−0.06	***	44.19%

predictive of lower depressive symptoms ($b = -0.22$, $p < .05$). This is suggestive evidence that God-mediated control has a significant indirect effect in the wisdom➔depressive symptoms relationship. In the first row of Table 3, we see this result confirmed with formal mediation analyses. God-mediated control has a significant indirect effect ($b = -0.04$, $Z = -2.46$, $p < .05$). Indeed, God-mediated control explains 25.75% of the relationship between wisdom and lower depressive symptoms. ➔

Model 3 tests whether trust in God as an additional mediating pathway. We again observe that the significant relationship between wisdom and lower depressive symptoms that we observed in Model 1 is reduced to non-significance ($b = 0.01$, $p > .05$). The results of the Sobel-Goodman mediation test shown in Table 3 also confirm this result. As shown in the second row, trust in God had a significant indirect effect ($b = -0.08$, $Z = -3.85$, $p < .001$). Relative to God-mediated control, trust in God explained more than twice the proportion of the relationship between wisdom and lower depressive symptoms (54.01%).

Finally, Model 4 introduced gratitude to God as our third mediating pathway of interest, without adjustment for God-mediated control nor trust in God. Consistent with our observations in Models 2 and 3, the introduction of this variable likewise reduces the association between wisdom and lower depressive symptoms to non-significance ($b = -0.01$, $p > .05$). Sobel-Goodman tests of mediation confirm this significant indirect effect through gratitude towards God ($b = -0.06$, $Z = -3.69$, $p < .001$). Gratitude to God also explained approximately 44% of the overall relationship between practical wisdom and lower depressive symptoms, net of all other study covariates, representing almost twice the magnitude of the practical wisdom➔God-mediated control➔depressive symptoms pathways and a similar magnitude to the same pathway through trust in God.

Altogether then, we observe support for Hypotheses 2, 3, and 4: each God-related construct (God-mediated control, trust in God, and gratitude towards God) was a significant mediator of the relationship between practical wisdom and depressive symptoms. However, we observed that in relative magnitude, trust in God had the strongest mediating pathway, followed by gratitude towards God and finally by God-mediated control. We return in the next section to reflect on this pattern findings.

Discussion

Humans have a desire to be wise to some degree so as to make decisions in both the short and long term that will optimize happiness. The last several decades have witnessed the topic of wisdom gaining momentum in the field of positive psychology (Glück et al., 2013). The study of the virtue of wisdom therefore highlights a rich intersection between psychology and religion (Krause & Hayward, 2015; Wink & Dillon, 2013). Both wisdom and spirituality are foundational to both philosophical and religious discourses, yet each is a profound and extremely complex construct with a myriad of nuances. Social scientists have been trying to grapple with each construct with some success, but their intertwined relationships remain obscure at best.

Recognizing this gap, this current study posited facets of religion, most fundamentally, one's relationship with God, as an explanatory mechanism linking wisdom with depression among older adults. We make two contributions to the literature. First, we show that practical wisdom, a master virtue essential for problem-solving (Schwartz & Sharpe, 2006), is associated with lower depressive symptoms in a sample of older adults. Our study improves on the majority of previous work in the wisdom and well-being literature has either considered general measures of negative affect (Etezadi & Pushkar, 2013) or life satisfaction (Grossmann et al., 2013; Le, 2011) without focusing specifically on depressive symptoms. That practical wisdom bears an inverse relationship with depressive symptoms further solidifies wisdom as a virtue with deep-seated linkages to well-being. As both Aristotle and St. Thomas Aquinas noted, wisdom was essential to the human condition (Kristjánsson, 2010). Practical wisdom may allow older adults to cope with adversity by drawing on past experience to overcome such hardships (Aldwin & Igarashi, 2015; Ardelt & Ferrari, 2014) and through engaging in processes of self-reflection where they may become more mindful and aware of their emotions (Ardelt, 2003). In their discussion of the "paradox" of wisdom and well-being, Ardelt and Jeste (2018) argue that seeing reality more might not automatically promote well-being, unless individuals are also able to develop the equanimity to accept their present reality and see beyond its immediate circumstances when confronted with adversity and hardship. It appears that practical wisdom, insofar as it helps people translate virtues into action (Schwartz & Sharpe, 2006), may also relate favorably to mental well-being.

Our second and more novel contribution to the literature was our documentation that three God-related constructs, God-mediated control, trust in God, and gratitude towards God in later life, each partially explained the relationship between wisdom and well-being. These findings were consistent with our expectations, but they hold significance for two reasons. First, as we reviewed at the outset of this study, the relationship between religion and wisdom has been plague by inconsistent findings, with some studies finding a significant relationship between the two (Krause & Hayward, 2014; Wink & Dillon, 2013) and others showing null associations or otherwise complex associations (Adamovová, 2013; Brezina & van Oudenhoven, 2012). We suggested that wisdom may be in fact be best conceptualized as the *precursor* to greater religiosity; indeed, in our conceptual framework, wisdom was thought to be causally prior to each God-related variable. We argued that wiser older adults may recognize the limitations of their own capacities and come to rely on God as a collaborative partner (Krause, 2005), trust in His plan (Krause, 2015), or be self-reflective enough to recognize and be grateful for all the gifts God has bestowed upon a person (Krause et al., 2014).

The relative magnitude of the three mediating pathways tested is suggestive of the processes that may be operating to connect wisdom with lower depressive symptoms among older adults. Trust in God explained over 50% of the association between wisdom and well-being, far exceeding that explained by God-mediated control and narrowly edging out gratitude to God. Why might this be? Wisdom may be the key to unlock placing one's unconditional trust in God, spurring a process of self-reflection that conjures up reminders of the utility of trusting God's plan. Placing such trust in God involves taking a risk that God will come through in a positive way and bestow through His grace the appropriate virtues to address a particular situation (e.g., humility when confronted with illness, or gratitude for the life of a deceased loved one). Being wise enough to trust in God may also help to quell fears about death, fueled by hope of the afterlife (Krause, 2015). Though God-mediated control beliefs was certainly also an important factor connecting wisdom to well-being, rely on God's assistance as an engaged, collaborative partner seems less tightly connected to wisdom than trusting a divine plan that once cannot see and is not immanently known. Wisdom may help people recognize the limits of their own abilities and as a result, they know that they can trust God to handle the things in life that they are not capable of handling on their own. God-mediated control can certainly have utility for individuals coping with stress (Krause, 2005, 2010; Upenieks & Ford-Robertson, 2022), but wisdom seems less central to getting older adults to this state of co-partnership with God that it does to trust that God will, in His own time and way, fulfill His promises.

Gratitude to God also shared a similarly strong explanatory pathway connecting wisdom to well-being as did trust in God. As secular constructs, wisdom and gratitude have been known to be positively related (Konig & Glück, 2013), as the self-reflective processes that are hallmarks of wisdom may generate feelings of gratitude to the source of one's gifts and resources. Wisdom also appears to promote greater feelings of gratitude towards God, believed to be the source of all good here on earth. Wiser older adults appear not to take their relationship with God, nor the gifts He has bestowed upon them, for granted. Gratitude to God may be an example of a virtue that would naturally flow from practical wisdom, helping individuals to effectively cope with stress in the process (Upenieks & Ford-Robertson, 2022), and ultimately serving as a resource that has protective benefits for mental health.

Taken together, our empirical tests of mediating pathways through measures that gauge the nature of older adults' relationships with God breaks new ground. Linking wisdom with God-mediated control, trust, and gratitude plays an important role in developing the literature because it provides one way to integrate these seemingly disparate measures into a larger, more comprehensive framework. Moreover, our study helps to clarify the otherwise murky relationship between religion and wisdom. It also demonstrates that Christian conceptions of God as a personal, divine being, the ultimate attachment figure who is an unconditional source of love and support for believers, may be a target of older adults who have cultivated practical wisdom. Wisdom appears to be largely motivated by higher needs, such as psychological growth and the need to achieve a sense of meaning and purpose in life (Grossmann et al., 2020). The pathway that we proposed of wisdom associating with greater trust in God, gratitude towards God, and beliefs in God-mediated control shows one way in which practical wisdom may re-focus the attention of older adults towards the divine in ways that draw them closer to God. Since the data in our study were provided by older adults, we would point to evidence that has suggested that people who originated from earlier cohorts in the United States are more deeply involved in religion than those who are currently younger (Krause, 2008). While the average individual becomes wiser with age (Baltes, 2004), we show here that wisdom is linked to well-being among our sample especially because it promotes more favorable relationships with the divine that place control of the outcomes in one's life as well as the focus of one's attention outside of individual control.

Limitations and future directions

While the findings from our study provide some useful insights, our study was limited in several respects. First and foremost, we relied on cross-sectional data, and as a result, the temporal ordering among the constructs in our conceptual model were based on theoretical considerations alone. We argued that wisdom was likely to promote stronger beliefs in God-mediated control, trust in God, and gratitude towards God, which in turn would associate with lower depressive symptoms. Alternative causal orderings could be proposed, where those with more God-mediated control, trust in God, and gratitude toward God may foster greater wisdom, or where lower depressive symptoms may foster a stronger relationship with God. These issues must be rigorously addressed with data that have been gathered at more than one time point.

Second, because we relied on a Christian sample, it is not possible to ascertain whether out findings would generalize to faith traditions beyond Christianity. We suspect that our findings would translate, given that Baltes (2004) suggests documents on wisdom date back to at least the third millennium before Christ. In addition, every major civilization and every faith tradition has devoted considerable thought to wisdom. Thus, what may differ between faith traditions is how wisdom is translated to greater well-being, perhaps through processes unrelated to one's relationship with a divine entity.

Third, it would be useful for future research to examine the relationship between wisdom and other measures of health and well-being, including physical health, functional disability, and acute and chronic health conditions, as well as the role of religious/spiritual factors in this pathway. We also need to understand more about the relationship between practical wisdom and other indicators of psychological well-being. For instance, it is plausible that greater practical wisdom may be associated with a greater sense of meaning in life as well as stronger feelings of personal mastery. Finally, it would be useful for future research to consider if there are potential subgroup variations in the conceptual model that we developed; for example, it could be important to consider if the relationship between wisdom and depressive symptoms, and the mediating role of the three God-related constructs assessed in this study, is different for older men or women, or for those of different racial backgrounds or with varying levels of educational attainment.

Conclusion

Wisdom is a values virtue concerning a deeper understanding of both the challenges and uncertainties that form the human experience. The attainment of wisdom is often thought to represent the pinnacle of human development and is generally viewed as one of the most important outcomes of the aging process (Ardelt, 2003). Our study has demonstrated that the relationship between wisdom and depressive symptoms in older adults is mediated by God-mediated control, trust in God, and gratitude in God. Religion is implicated in this process to the extent that wise individuals have better, more developed relationships with God, allowing them first and foremost to trust in His plan for their lives, and expertly interact with their environment to maximize well-being. Considered as a whole, our study advances the field of research at the intersection of wisdom, religion, and well-being by suggesting, and finding evidence in support of, possible psychological mechanisms housed in one's relationships with God that may underlie the salubrious association between wisdom and well-being in later life. As Jonathan Haidt notes in his book, *The Happiness Hypothesis* (2007, pg.39), wise people are able to achieve a life balance which "corresponds to the famous 'serenity prayer': God, grant me the serenity to accept the things I cannot change, courage to change the things I can, and the wisdom to know the difference."

Disclosure statement

No potential conflict of interest was reported by the author(s).

Funding

This research was support by a grant from the John Templeton Foundation and the United States Department of Health and Human Services, National Institutes of Health, National Institute on Aging (Grant RO1 AG009221).

References

Adamovová, L. (2013). Wise religiosity: The relationship between religiosity and wisdom moderated by personality traits. *Studia psychologica*, *55*(3), 181–194. https://doi.org/10.21909/sp.2013.03.634

Ai, A. L., Park, C. L., Huang, B., Rodgers, W., & Tice, T. N. (2007). Psychosocial mediation of religious coping styles: A study of short-term psychological distress following cardiac surgery. *Personality & Social Psychology Bulletin*, *33*(6), 867–882. https://doi.org/10.1177/0146167207301008

Aldwin, C. M., & Igarashi, H. (2015). Successful, optimal, and resilient aging: A psychosocial perspective. In P. A. Lichtenberg & B. T. Mast (Eds.), *APA handbook of clinical geropsychology* (pp. 331–359). American Psychological Association. https://doi.org/10.1037/14458-014.s

Ardelt, M. (1997). Wisdom and life satisfaction in old age. *The Journals of Gerontology Series B, Psychological Sciences and Social Sciences, 52*(1), 15–27. https://doi.org/10.1093/geronb/52B.1.P15

Ardelt, M. (2003). Empirical assessment of a three-dimensional wisdom scale. *Research on Aging, 25*(3), 275–324. https://doi.org/10.1177/0164027503025003004

Ardelt, M. (2011). The measurement of wisdom: A commentary on taylor, bates, and webster's comparison of the SAWS and 3D-WS. *Experimental Aging Research, 37*(2), 241–255. https://doi.org/10.1080/0361073X.2011.554509

Ardelt, M. (2019). Wisdom and well-being. In R. J. Sternberg & J. Glück (Eds.), *The Cambridge handbook of wisdom* (pp. 602–625). Cambridge University Press. https://doi.org/10.1017/9781108568272.028

Ardelt, M., Achenbaum, W. A., & Oh, H. (2013). The paradoxical nature of personal wisdom and its relation to human development in the reflective, cognitive, and affective domains. In M. Ferrari & N. M. Weststrate (Eds.), *The scientific study of personal wisdom: From contemplative traditions to neuroscience* (pp. 265–295). Springer.

Ardelt, M., Ai, A. L., & Eichenberger, S. E. (2008). In search for meaning: The differential role of religion for middle-aged and older persons diagnosed with a life-threatening illness. *Journal of Religion, Spirituality & Aging, 20*(4), 288–312.

Ardelt, M., & Edwards, C. A. (2016). Wisdom at the end of life: An analysis of mediating and moderating relations between wisdom and subjective well-being. *The Journals of Gerontology Series B, Psychological Sciences and Social Sciences, 71*(3), 502–513. https://doi.org/10.1093/geronb/gbv051

Ardelt, M., & Ferrari, M. (2014). Wisdom and emotions. In P. Verhaeghen & C. Hertzog (Eds.), *The oxford handbook of emotion, social cognition, and problem solving in adulthood* (pp. 256–272). Oxford University Press.

Ardelt, M., & Jeste, D. V. (2018). Wisdom and hard times: The ameliorating effect of wisdom on the negative association between adverse life events and well-being. *The Journals of Gerontology: Series B, 73*(8), 1374–1383.

Aristotle. (2000). In R. Crisp (Ed.), *Nicomachean ethics.*Cambridge University Press.

Baltes, P. B. (2004). *Wisdom as orchestration of mind and virtue.* Unpublished manuscript: http://library.mpib-berlin.mpg.de/ft/pb/PB_Wisdom_2004.pdf.

Baltes, P. B., & Staudinger, U. M. (2000). Wisdom: A metaheuristic (pragmatic) to orchestrate mind and virtue toward excellence. *The American Psychologist, 55*(1), 122–136. https://doi.org/10.1037/0003-066X.55.1.122

Berger, P. (1969). *The social reality of religion.* Penguin.

Bergsma, A., & Ardelt, M. (2012). Self-reported wisdom and happiness: An empirical investigation. *Journal of Happiness Studies, 13*(3), 481–499. https://doi.org/10.1007/s10902-011-9275-5

Brezina, I., & Van Oudenhoven, J. P. (2012). Do national cultures or religions shape conceptions of wisdom? *Studia psychologica, 54*(4), 299–310.

Clemence, A., Karmaniola, A., Green, E. G., & Spini, D. (2007). Disturbing life events and wellbeing after 80 years of age: A longitudinal comparison of survivors and the deceased over five years. *Ageing & Society, 27*(2), 195–213. https://doi.org/10.1017/S0144686X06005630

Davis, D. E., Worthington, E. L., Jr., Hook, J. N., & Hill, P. C. (2013). Research on religion/spirituality and forgiveness: A meta-analytic review. *Psychology of Religion and Spirituality, 5* (4), 233–241. https://doi.org/10.1037/a0033637

Emmons, R. A., & Kneezel, T. T. (2005). Giving thanks: Spiritual and religious correlates of gratitude. *Journal of Psychology & Christianity, 24*(2), 140–148.

Erikson, E. H. (1982). *The life cycle completed.* Norton.

Etezadi, S., & Pushkar, D. (2013). Why are wise people happier? An explanatory model of wisdom and emotional well-being in older adults. *Journal of Happiness Studies, 14*(3), 929–950. https://doi.org/10.1007/s10902-012-9362-2

Fadardi, J. S., & Azadi, Z. (2017). The relationship between trust-in-God, positive and negative affect, and hope. *Journal of Religion and Health, 56*(3), 796–806. https://doi.org/10.1007/s10943-015-0134-2

Glück, J. (2018). Measuring wisdom: Existing approaches, continuing challenges, and new developments. *The Journals of Gerontology: Series B, 73*(8), 1393–1403. https://doi.org/10.1093/geronb/gbx140

Glück, J., König, S., Naschenweng, K., Redzanowski, U., Dorner, L., Straßer, I., & Wiedermann, W. (2013). How to measure wisdom: Content, reliability, and validity of five measures. *Frontiers in Psychology, 4*, 405. https://doi.org/10.3389/fpsyg.2013.00405

Grossmann, I., Na, J., Varnum, M. E., Kitayama, S., & Nisbett, R. E. (2013). A route to well-being: Intelligence versus wise reasoning. *Journal of Experimental Psychology General, 142*(3), 944–953. https://doi.org/10.1037/a0029560

Grossmann, I., Weststrate, N. M., Ardelt, M., Brienza, J. P., Dong, M., Ferrari, M., Fournier, M. A., Hu, C. S., Nusbaum, H. C., & Vervaeke, J. (2020). The science of wisdom in a polarized world: Knowns and unknowns. *Psychological Inquiry, 31*(2), 103–133. https://doi.org/10.1080/1047840X.2020.1750917

Hayes, A. F. (2013). *Mediation, moderation, and conditional process analysis.* (Hayes A. F., Ed.). Guilford Press.

Hood, R. W., Jr., Hill, P. C., & Spilka, B. (2009). *The psychology of religion: An empirical approach.* Guilford Press.

Jackson, B. R., & Bergeman, C. S. (2011). How does religiosity enhance well-being? The role of perceived control. *Psychology of Religion and Spirituality, 3*(2), 149–161. https://doi.org/10.1037/a0021597

Judge, T. A., Ilies, R., & Dimotakis, N. (2010). Are health and happiness the product of wisdom? The relationship of general mental ability to educational and occupational attainment, health, and well-being. *The Journal of Applied Psychology, 95*(3), 454–468. https://doi.org/10.1037/a0019084

Kirkpatrick, L. A. (2005). *Attachment, evolution, and the psychology of religion.* Guilford Press.

König, S., & Glück, J. (2013). Individual differences in wisdom conceptions: Relationships to gratitude and wisdom. *International Journal of Aging & Human Development, 77*(2), 127–147.

Kraaij, V., Arensman, E., & Spinhoven, P. (2002). Negative life events and depression in elderly persons: A meta-analysis. *The Journals of Gerontology Series B, Psychological Sciences and Social Sciences, 57*(1), 87–P94. https://doi.org/10.1093/geronb/57.1.P87

Krause, N. (2002). A comprehensive strategy for developing closed-ended survey items for use in studies of older adults. *The Journals of Gerontology Series B, Psychological Sciences and Social Sciences, 57*(5), S263–274. https://doi.org/10.1093/geronb/57.5.S263

Krause, N. (2005). God-mediated control and psychological well-being in late life. *Research on Aging, 27*(2), 136–164. https://doi.org/10.1177/0164027504270475

Krause, N. (2006). Exploring the stress-buffering effects of church-based and secular social support on self-rated health in late life. *Journals of Gerontology, Series B: Psychological Sciences & Social Sciences, 61*(1), S35–43.

Krause, N. (2008). *Aging in the church: how social relationships affect health.* Templeton Foundation Press.

Krause, N. (2009). Religious involvement, gratitude, and change in depressive symptoms over time. *The International Journal for the Psychology of Religion*, *19*(3), 155–172. https://doi.org/10.1080/10508610902880204

Krause, N. (2010). God-mediated control and change in self-rated health. *The International Journal for the Psychology of Religion*, *20*(4), 267–287. https://doi.org/10.1080/10508619.2010.507695

Krause, N. (2012). Religious involvement, humility, and change in self-rated health over time. *Journal of Psychology and Theology*, *40*(3), 199–210. https://doi.org/10.1177/009164711204000303

Krause, N. (2015). Trust in God and psychological distress: Exploring variations by religious affiliation. *Mental Health, Religion & Culture*, *18*(4), 235–245. https://doi.org/10.1080/13674676.2015.1021311

Krause, N. (2016). Assessing the relationships among wisdom, humility, and life satisfaction. *Journal of Adult Development*, *23*(3), 140–149. https://doi.org/10.1007/s10804-016-9230-0

Krause, N., Bruce, D., Hayward, R. D., & Woolever, C. (2014). Gratitude to god, self-rated health, and depressive symptoms. *Journal for the Scientific Study of Religion*, *53*(2), 341–355. https://doi.org/10.1111/jssr.12110

Krause, N., Emmons, R. A., Ironson, G., & Hill, P. C. (2017). General feelings of gratitude, gratitude to God, and hemoglobin A1c: Exploring variations by gender. *The Journal of Positive Psychology*, *12*(6), 639–650. https://doi.org/10.1080/17439760.2017.1326520

Krause, N., & Hayward, R. D. (2014). Religious involvement, practical wisdom, and self-rated health. *Journal of Aging and Health*, *26*(4), 540–558. https://doi.org/10.1177/0898264314524437

Krause, N., & Hayward, R. D. (2015). Assessing whether practical wisdom and awe of God are associated with life satisfaction. *Psychology of Religion and Spirituality*, *7*(1), 51–59. https://doi.org/10.1037/a0037694

Kristjánsson, K. (2010). Positive psychology, happiness, and virtue: The troublesome conceptual issues. *Review of General Psychology*, *14*(4), 296–310. https://doi.org/10.1037/a0020781

Le, T. N. (2011). Life satisfaction, openness value, self-transcendence, and wisdom. *Journal of Happiness Studies*, *12*(2), 171–182. https://doi.org/10.1007/s10902-010-9182-1

Levenson, M. R., Jennings, P. A., Aldwin, C. M., & Shiraishi, R. W. (2005). Self-transcendence: Conceptualization and measurement. *International Journal of Aging & Human Development*, *60*(2), 127–143. https://doi.org/10.2190/XRXM-FYRA-7U0X-GRC0

Linley, P. A. (2003). Positive adaptation to trauma: Wisdom as both process and outcome. *Journal of Traumatic Stress*, *16*(6), 601–610. https://doi.org/10.1023/B:JOTS.0000004086.64509.09

Lundberg, C. D. (2010). *Unifying truths of the world's religions*. Heavenlight Press.

Pace, M. (2020). Trusting to inspire trustworthiness. Syntheses. Advance online publication. https://doi.org/10.1007/s11229-020-02840-8.

Pargament, K. I., Magyar-russell, G. M., & Murray-swank, N. A. (2005). The sacred and the search for significance: Religion as a unique process. *The Journal of Social Issues*, *61*(4), 665–687. https://doi.org/10.1111/j.1540-4560.2005.00426.x

Pargament, K. I., Tarakeshwar, N., Ellison, C. G., & Wulff, K. M. (2001). Religious coping among the religious: The relationships between religious coping and well-being in a national sample of presbyterian clergy, elders, and members. *Journal for the Scientific Study cf Religion*, *40*(3), 497–513. https://doi.org/10.1111/0021-8294.00073

Radloff, L. S. (1977). The CES-D scale: A self-report depression scale for research in the general population. *Applied Psychological Measurement*, *1*(3), 385–401. https://doi.org/10.1177/014662167700100306

Rosmarin, D. H., Pargament, K. I., & Mahoney, A. (2009). The role of religiousness in anxiety, depression, and happiness in a Jewish community sample: A preliminary investigation. *Mental Health, Religion & Culture, 12*(2), 97–113. https://doi.org/10.1080/13674670802321933

Schieman, S., Pudrovska, T., & Milkie, M. A. (2005). The sense of divine control and the self-concept: A study of race differences in late life. *Research on Aging, 27*(2), 165–196. https://doi.org/10.1177/0164027504270489

Schwartz, B., & Sharpe, K. E. (2006). Practical wisdom: Aristotle meets positive psychology. *Journal of Happiness Studies, 7*(3), 377–395. https://doi.org/10.1007/s10902-005-3651-y

Staudinger, U. M., & Glück, J. (2011). Psychological wisdom research: Commonalities and differences in a growing field. *Annual Review of Psychology, 62*(1), 215–241. https://doi.org/10.1146/annurev.psych.121208.131659

Taylor, M., Bates, G., & Webster, J. D. (2011). Comparing the psychometric properties of two measures of wisdom: Predicting forgiveness and psychological well-being with the Self-Assessed Wisdom Scale (SAWS) and the three-dimensional Wisdom Scale (3D-WS). *Experimental Aging Research, 37*(2), 129–141. https://doi.org/10.1080/0361073X.2011.554508

Tennen, H., & Affleck, G. (2002). Benefit-finding and benefit re- minding. In C. R. Snyder & S. J. Lopez (Eds.), *Handbook of positive psychology* (pp. 548–597). Oxford University Press.

Upenieks, L., & Ford-Robertson, J. (2022). Give thanks in all circumstances? Gratitude toward god and health in later life after major life stressors. *Research on Aging, 44*(5–6), 392–404. https://doi.org/10.1177/01640275211033914

Walsh, R. (2015). What is wisdom? Cross-cultural and cross-disciplinary syntheses. *Review of General Psychology, 19*(3), 278–293. https://doi.org/10.1037/gpr0000045

Ward, K. (1994). *Religion and revelation: A theology of revelation in the world's religions.* Oxford University Press.

Webster, J. D., Westerhof, G. J., & Bohlmeijer, E. T. (2014). Wisdom and mental health across the lifespan. *The Journals of Gerontology Series B, Psychological Sciences and Social Sciences, 69*(2), 209–218. https://doi.org/10.1093/geronb/gbs121

Weststrate, N. M., & Glück, J. (2017). Hard-earned wisdom: Exploratory processing of difficult life experience is positively associated with wisdom. *Developmental Psychology, 53*(4), 800–814. https://doi.org/10.1037/dev0000286

Wink, P., & Dillon, M. (2013). Religion, spirituality, and personal wisdom: A tale of two types. In M. Ferrari & N. Weststrate (Eds.), *The scientific study of personal wisdom* (pp. 165–189). Springer.

Zagzebski, L. (1998). The virtues of god and the foundations of ethics. *Faith and Philosophy, 15* (4), 538–553. https://doi.org/10.5840/faithphil199815446

Finitude and eternity: mental companions of soulful aging?

Frieder R. Lang

ABSTRACT
It is a well-known finding that perceived finitude plays a critical role in the process of aging. The current article addressed how perceptions of finitude and eternity contribute to a soulful aging experience. Infinity is introduced as a temporal concept involving endurance and everlasting existence of time that marks the opposite end of finitude of a human life. Eternity, in contrast, relates to a timeless concept going beyond time without beginning or ending characterized by omnipresence. While the soul reflects eternity, the aging experience pertains to finitude. I suggest that the experience of soulful aging requires an integrative balance between reflections and perceptions of eternity and finitude. This involves a reappraisal of personal finitude into one of the three possible perceptions of infinity, that is, one that views infinity as not including the self, one that views infinity in being commemorated, and one that construes infinity as a possible afterlife of a soul. Conversing personal finitude into perspectives of infinity and eternity may also contribute to positive outcomes in the process of aging.

> For whoever wants to save their life will lose it, but whoever loses their life for me will find it. What good will it be for someone to gain the whole world, yet forfeit their soul? Or what can anyone give in exchange for their soul?
>
> *Matthew 16:25–26*
> *New International Version*

When my friend Andrew Achenbaum invited me to contribute a piece on soulful aging, I recklessly agreed with a mix of hubris, honor, and sympathy. Who am I to write about the soul in aging experience? Are 40 years of studying psychology or 30 years of studying aging helping to resolve the task? I sensed not at all. Maybe 60 years of survival on earth helped me a little. In the following, I argue that perceptions of finitude and eternity dynamically interplay in the aging process. Infinity is used here as a temporal concept involving endurance and everlasting existence of time that marks the opposite end of finitude of a human life. Eternity, in contrast, relates to a timeless concept going beyond time without beginning or ending and that is characterized by omnipresence.

Theology informs us about eternity. From the health and life sciences, we are informed that human existence is finite. Consequently, the science of finitude cannot easily be linked up with theological science of eternal spirit: While the latter relates to soul, the former relates to mind, self, or psyche that is limited by nature and in time. In this vein, the term "soulful aging" constitutes an oxymoron, because human aging is defined by finitude, whereas soul is defined by divine timelessness. It seems merely impossible to refer to the phenomena of finitude, and eternity simultaneously within the same context. While finitude involves a theory of (aging) self, mind, or psyche, eternity refers to the idea of redeeming the soul. As it goes in life, and against all odds I set myself the task to write exactly about this oxymoronic thought although it can hardly be resolved. Why is this the case? It is because my perspective is narrow and limited from start as I own not more than the gerontological view of an inveterate aging psychologist. Why do I still try? It is because I own the gerontological view of an inveterate aging psychologist.

The blessings of perceiving finitude

> He has made everything beautiful in its time. He has also set eternity in the human heart; yet no one can fathom what God has done from beginning to end. I know that there is nothing better for people than to be happy and to do good while they live. That each of them may eat and drink and find satisfaction in all their toil – this is the gift of God. I know that everything God does will endure forever; nothing can be added to it, and nothing taken from it.
>
> *Ecclesiastes 3:1, 11–14*
> *New International Version*

In aging research, considerations on perceived finitude have become proliferate and productive to advance our understanding of aging changes, while the roles of infinity and eternity in human aging appear to remain neglected with few exceptions. What difference does it make in the aging process how individuals approach the idea of timelessness, infinity, or eternity? It may appear to be a truism that perspectives on time differ by discipline: an astrophysicist may think of the endless time as a black hole, while a geologist may think of the endless transformation of inorganic substance, and an evolutionary biologist thinks about infinite variety and continuous replication. A theologist refers to the timeless existence of the eternal God. In Ecclesiastes 3:1 it says, "there is a time for everything". I believe that this verse reflects a fundamental wisdom for humanity. Doesn't this also imply that there is a time for finitude, and a time for eternity? Can we imagine both in one life? The puzzle may be resolved when differentiating two levels of observation.

On a *personal level* perceiving finitude reflects an awareness that there exists an ending of one's life on earth. The contents of such thoughts may play a decisive role when experiencing some of the burden, hurts, or defeats of aging decrement in later life. Thus, understanding the limitation of one's remaining time in life is helpful to focus on how to enhance, protect, or savor purpose in life for the time that is left. In this context, the idea of eternity may entail a promise, a relief, or a threat to meaning. The promise may involve a hope of an end to burden and pains in this life, the relief may pertain to the idea of a putative salvation, and the threat may occur when imagining a possible infinity of being.

On a *suprapersonal level*, in contrast, the idea of finitude points to the heritage of humanity and the implied contract between successive generations to protect and preserve the creation. The ending of one involves the beginning of one other. Endings are thus required to enable the development of novelty in human society. When there is no ending there is no succession. There are many active and productive ways of passing on, supporting, giving way to others, and serving to keep the meaning. With a suprapersonal view of finitude the idea of infinity seems more conceivable.

The personal level focuses on the self, the suprapersonal level widens the perspective away from self towards human existence in total. It can happen that a person vacillates between the two perspectives. It is a quest that is not easy to resolve: Is the ending of my life relevant only to myself, to my loved ones and kindred, to society, or to life in general? What does "relevant" imply? The attempt to answer humbly may fail, because the task is not in deciding for the one or the other, the task is on seeking an integration of the many ways of dealing with finitude. One blessing of perceived finiteness in life is that it may help to reinterpret and cognitively restructure one's personal limitation in life. I argue that the experience of soulful aging requires an integrative balance between these two levels of thinking about finitude and infinity, and a reappraisal of personal finitude into one of the three possible perceptions of infinity, that is, one that construes infinity as a possible afterlife of a soul, one that views infinity in being commemorated or remembered, and one that views infinity as not including the self. Building on a rich psychological literature, I refer to such reappraisal of personal finitude as *transcendental*, *relational*, and *transformational* future perspective.

Is there a blessing in the thought of an eternal soul?

The soul is an elephant in a securely locked psychological closet.

When I enrolled in psychology at university as a young person, I had read already quite a few texts about human soul in the works of Sigmund Freud and Erik H. Erikson, who used the German word "*Seele*" (*soul*) for the Greek word "*Psyche*" to describe the structures of the conscious and unconscious mind. In my first year in university, I quickly learned that psychology does not speak of the "*Psyche*" but rather reflects on the human mind, perception, cognition, and affect. After some more years of study, I eventually understood that philosophers and psychologists like *George H. Mead* or *William James* defined the *self* as an individual's subjective experience perceiving this individual's own mind: The self is what a person implies when saying, "Me". It took me a few more days to learn that humanistic ideas of self-actualization in the works of Abraham Maslow (1958) or Charlotte Bühler (1968) are not so far away from seeking salvation during one's limited lifetime. About one decade later, experimental psychologists began to detect that there is more than consciousness in the human mind, and that implicit non-conscious processing of the mind is invisible although it can be traced experimentally. There is implicit, automatic, non-conscious neurological activity that may or may not regulate, determine, or reflect our free will. There is no good reason to doubt that our free will is serving the self, but yes, we do not know whether the free will is serving the soul. However, the soul appears to be selfless obviously not selfish.

The *self*, the *mind*, the *consciousness*, or the *psyche* are scientific terms that do not include the soul as an entity. There is no definition of soul in psychology that goes beyond the mind-body problem of whether thinking or feeling can be separated and isolated from physiology in the organism (Rank, 1996; Westphal, 2016). What can be told about "*aging with soul*" that is different from what is known about aging of self, aging of mind, or aging identity? And how is *soulful aging* different from cognitive aging, mindful aging, or positive aging?

In aging research, the *self* has become an almost empty shorthand for any aspect of behavior, thought, cognition, or affect in the aging process that cannot be observed directly and therefore requires a person's narrative or report. The self has become a meaningless term in psychological and behavioral literature pertaining to all phenomena of the mind and to subjective experience.

There has been the notion of an "*age-less self*" (Kaufman, 1986), describing the subjective experience of continuity and oneself being the same person regardless of current age. Such experience of self-continuity may be helpful in the process of understanding and savoring meaning in life. Self-continuity relies on autobiographical narration and coherence of the stories that we like to tell from the remembered past (Bluck & Alea, 2008). In addition, there is the concept of a mind reflecting human cognition and capability and being challenged in the aging process. For example, in Ellen Langer's epochal work (1992), mindful aging was described as a strategy of counteracting aging challenges by focusing on the here and now. Mindful aging takes advantage of the temporal limitations of life: When focusing on the here and now our mind's resources can bring out the best performance, and we may even trick the passage of time as Langer did in her phenomenal and not replicated counterclockwise study (Langer, 2009): In this study, a group of 10 older men were made to relive a time 20 years ago as if it were today, and who behaved and felt more youthfully at the time.

Neither mind nor self nor psyche appear to speak to the idea of a soul that may be filling or fulfilling my aging experience. What, or where is the soul in all this? The nomological network that unfolds from the terms of soul, self, mind, psyche, and consciousness is reminiscent of the allegory of the blind men and the elephant describing the limitations of human cognition, perception, and understanding. The allegory goes as follows:

> *A group of blind men heard that a strange animal, called an elephant, had been brought to the town, but none of them were aware of its shape and form. Out of curiosity, they said: "We must inspect and know it by touch, of which we are capable". So, they sought it out, and when they found it, they groped about it. The first person, whose hand landed on the trunk, said, "This being is like a thick snake". For another one whose hand reached its ear, it seemed like a kind of fan. As for another person, whose hand was upon its leg, said, the elephant is a pillar like a tree-trunk. The blind man who placed his hand upon its side said the elephant, "is a wall". Another who felt its tail, described it as a rope. The last felt its tusk, stating the elephant is that which is hard, smooth and like a spear. (Wikipedia (2022), retrieved on Feb 14, 2023, https://en.wikipedia.org/wiki/Blind_men_and_an_elephant).*

In my scientific career, I was honored to attend a few lectures of esteemed scholars who liked to use this allegory above when introducing the complexity of their (psychological) topic to their audience. In these lessons, the scholars would typically choose a pictorial representation of an elephant surrounded by some obviously blind very old white-bearded or grey-haired men (mostly an image from an antique Indian or Chinese source). In all these cases, I wondered why the presenters would illustrate the perception of a blind person with a picture showing what this blind person cannot see. I believe that any attempt to illustrate the idea of this parable with a picture showing an elephant counteracts the parable's actual meaning and true purpose. It is as easy as this: do not try to illustrate what can only be imagined as invisible. Does this remind anyone of the second commandment?

The soul in soulful aging resembles an invisible elephant that blind older men try to grasp or explore from different angles: one may think it is the aging self, another one may think it's the aging mind, and a third one calls it the aging brain, a fourth, fifth, and sixth one refers to it as psyche, consciousness, or spirit of aging. They all may agree in one commonality, that is, the phenomenon at stake remains invisible. And even if neurologist eagerly continue with trying to locate or materialize this phenomenon, the observable or physical substance of what we are seeking to grasp and describe in words has not been found.

When I was a young boy (unaware of being a psychologist one day) I remember that my father, a professor of botany, once told us at a family's dinner table about the early idea that the soul is in the human body somewhere between the stomach and the lung at the place of the diaphragm. Perhaps there was a belief that the muscle that is responsible for contraction of the lung and making us breath in and out is the miracle of the soul. I am not sure whether my father, a scientist and evolutionary biologist, was aware of having referred to Ancient Greek thought about the soul. I surely wasn't at that time, but I remember how curious and eager I became to learn more.

More than 50 years later, I do not think that scientific knowledge about the soul has grown much since Ancient Greek. The soul is a ubiquitous oddity and a constant in human thinking. There is only one characteristic that I believe is unique to the soul in contrast to the mind, psyche, consciousness, or self: it is the idea of timelessness and infinity.

The mind like the self can be analyzed experimentally with ever-growing brilliant methodology, and the, soul, however, remains invisible to any attempt of exposure or revelation. Interestingly though it seems that getting older may involve a likelihood of getting close to the meaning and understanding of soul. That is my starting point on the quest for an aging soul. I argue that it is about a transcending of the personal to the suprapersonal level, away from finitude to timeless, unlimited thought that I refer to as conversion of one's limited personal future.

Three views on the finitude of life

Over the past decades, gerontologists like me were eager to learn about the psychological implications and consequences of perceiving finitude. Becoming older involves getting closer to a lifetime's ending (Lang & Carstensen, 2002). Understanding such endings may change our priorities and how we approach the tasks and challenges of today and of tomorrow (John & Lang, 2015). Increasing longevity challenges a person's will to live, and how the person valuates late life. Getting older involves a thought that living much longer may not be always as desirable as young adults may hope, and motivation for living longer becomes more strongly depending on one's immediate life situation and health (Lang & Rupprecht, 2019). Feeling nearer to one's own death may naturally turn one's perspective towards the question: what will the next day bring?

However, such a focus towards the presence may not be comparable to a fresh mindful focus on "here and now" as Langer (1992) had in mind. It may rather reflect an examining, cautious, and daring concern about one's outlook. Perhaps, this is accompanied by a thought about the end and what may come after such an inevitable ending, for oneself, one's loved ones and for humanity. What will happen when I am not there? All the many personal losses that occurred during my lifetime inform me about what has been there after all dear lost grands, friends, mentors, and colleagues have gone, and despite this there is no knowledge about what has come after that I can call mine. I sense a vibrant fluctuation in my own thinking about all the possible perspectives on how life goes on beyond the fact that life will always go one for any other person. There is no truth on this issue that can be proven during a lifetime. But there is more knowledge than this. There are at least three fundamental views on infinity that can and should be differentiated: a transcendent, a relational, and a transformational perspective.

The transcendent perspective on timeless infinity is the one that may heal our wounds in times of despair as it promises some relief in the afterlife that we may even sense already on this side. The transcendence refers to the eternal promise that there is a greater purpose than the one that emerge from my narrow mind and limited wisdom. The transcendent perspective on eternity includes the hope that my existence did not just arise out of banal arbitrariness and chance. I have enjoyed reading the works of Albert Camus, Jean Paul Sartre, and Simone de Beauvoir in my emerging adulthood for exactly this reason: it confronted me with the bittersweet possibility of my existence as a purely ontogenetic being. It may not be surprising that there is no faster avenue to the holy spirit than denying it; it is what psychologists have termed an "ironic process" (Wegner, 1987). Any thought of eternity is hard to ignore. Transcendent perspectives are naturally triggering ironic processes about a possible salvation and healing of the self. This may also be reminiscent of Tornstam's (2005) work on Gerotranscendence that refers to a "cosmic dimension", which may involve ways of conversing personal finitude into perspectives on infinity. In similar ways Zimbardo and Boyd (2008, pp. 172–173) referred to transcendental future time perspective as one that " . . . *extends from the death of physical body to infinity* . . . ", which then " . . . *encompasses different events that include divine judgment, reunion with dead loved ones, eternal life, achieving oneness with nature, reincarnation, and the end of poverty, pain, and suffering.*" (pp. 172–173). In these notions the idea of transcending also involves a conversion of reality on earth into an ideal other world. It becomes clear that, transcendent perspectives on a timeless infinity reflect heterogeneity, diversity, and individuality rather than conformity or normativity. I believe this reflects a quest of meaning rather than a puzzle to be solved, it reflects the futile search for wisdom since wisdom cannot be attained by aspiring it. In the process of aging and when time remaining in life is running out, finitude may become more of a companion in everyday life, a thought that may affect one's decisions, attitudes, preferences, and behaviors.

The relational perspective on timeless infinity resembles transformational thought with adding the self as mediated through personal relationships or family. It pertains to the idea of one's soul continuing to exist as long as one is remembered in the thought or prayers of others. The relational view involves a conditional eternity. It depends on being loved and leaving a trace of one's life in the lives of others. Again, there may be extremes in such relational thought towards one's future. A low end may be represented in the idea of leaving a will that regulates one's material or spiritual inheritance for one's surviving dependents (and their dependents). A "high-end" perspective may be expressed when one seeks to leave a legacy combined with generativity and generosity.

Relational perspectives on infinity may become comprehensive when thinking of those people that one has lost in a lifetime: I can think of any dear friend or colleague, and the many beloved family members that I have lost in my life. Such remembering is a wonderful and poignant experience when it occurs. The moment I think back of a lost person, a dear face, a fond memory, or warm sentiment come to my mind, and it is not even hard to imagine that this very same person could still be around somewhere next door. If I concentrate myself, I can remember a sound of a laughter, a voice or I can remember an odor. In the first generation, the lost ones are still lively in our thoughts, but it is not over once I am gone. There exist recollections of all those people that have lived long before I was born that continue to be remembered at family celebrations, commemorative events, and festivities. The relational perspective on eternity is I believe an underestimated and unique human capability that entails the fundaments of our existence, hopes and fears, grief, and joy, poignancy and yearning, desire, and melancholia, the myriad of my lifelong experience projected into the future of all those who may have missed me or are perhaps feeling relieve when I am gone. I cannot know about eternity in relationships when I am gone, but I can try to influence the ways in which I am commemorated. When we become aware of our relational eternity, it may change the way we interact with others and how we approach our close or loved ones in daily life: What does it mean to understand the feeling it may cause when one has left? The conversion of one's finitude involves a focus on caring for others here and today. It reminds us of Langer´s idea of mindfulness with those we feel close to. The relational perspective on finitude bears and embraces the idea of an affective focus on advancing our most positive experiences in our actual social worlds (Carstensen & Meeks, 2021).

Finally, *the transformational perspective* occurs when thinking about timeless infinity as not including the self, a world that continues to exist after one has gone, a world without myself. The transformational perspective reflects a purely subjective, not factual perspective on meaning in life after one's life has ended, a humble self-less infinity. The obvious challenge of this thought lies in the oxymoronic imagination of oneself leaving traces that reach beyond oneself. The transformation may also remind of a generative attitude towards future generations and a desire for immortality (Wakefield, 1998). Transforming the understanding of one's limitation into the infinite opportunities of humanity involves a suprapersonal perspective, which may serve the process of achieving ego-integrity in the sense of Erikson (1985). One may also ask whether there is any relevance to this question at all considering one's possible non-existence: Is it important to know that life of others goes on after one's own life has ended? I see at least two opposing responses to this question marking opposite poles of one dimension: The extreme low end of such a perspective entails a solipsistic thought of "*après moi le deluge*" that expresses no interest in life beyond the limit of one's personal lifetime. An extreme high end of transformational perspective may be reflected, for example, in an altruistic struggle for justice, or an uncompromising moral integrity and ethical conduct. An archetypical instance of such high-end transformational perspective is expressed in a famous proverb once attributed to Martin Luther by the German protestant bishop Hans Lilje (1899-1977): *"If I knew that tomorrow was the end of the world, I would plant an apple tree today"*. It refers to the quest for meaning of life, which can help us not to give up in times of despair. It is the flickering candlelight of the search for meaning that nourishes and encourages a person's will to live.

Conclusion and outlook

To conclude, there are three possible ways of responding to and dealing with personal finitude in life that can be identified based on an abundance of empirical and theoretical literature in the field of gerontology and aging psychology. Several questions arise from such considerations. One is, how the transcendental, relational, and transformational conversion of personal finitude interplay. Can they be distinguished empirically? Perhaps more importantly, how do conversions of personal finitude contribute to soulful aging, and perhaps to positive aging? What are the possible consequences of conversing personal finitude into either a perspective of eternity or cosmic transcendence, a perspective of caring, loving, and giving to close persons, or an accepting, integrative and benevolent understanding that others' lives go on without oneself. There exists some preliminary empirical evidence for positive effects for each of these three perceptual conversions of personal finitude (e.g., Hösch et al., 2023; Lang & Carstensen, 2002; Lang & Rupprecht, 2019; Lu et al., 2018).

The subjective conversion of personal finitude into a cognitively restructured mental state builds on acceptance that paves the way for imagination of infinity, transcendental thinking, generativity, or symbolic immortality. Accepting the limits of life is at the core of soulful aging as it allows to understand the omnipresence of eternity involves here and now. This may serve a relational perspective on finitude, and it may also advance a transformational perspective towards next generations. This may also involve a complex integration of seemingly opposing states of both presence and absence, immediacy and eternity, or self-commitment and connectedness. It is about the remaining time left, and about what comes after while focusing on here and now. When there is pain the transcendental thought may entail relief, when there is fear the benevolence of others can smooth the waters, and when there is doubt, it may help to draw a track in the sand or to plant a tree. The different ways of converting personal finitude also reflect responses to constraints, challenges, and limitations that arise within human societies around the world related to climate change, disaster, war, or poverty. It is suggested that the three types of subjective conversion of personal finitude (i.e., transcendental, relational, and transformational) can be distinguished analytically and empirically, while also contributing differently to positive aging. Soulful aging both requires and advances such conversion of personal finitude into meaning of life.

Acknowledgment

I express my gratitude to Andrew Achenbaum and Yaeji Kim-Knauss for invaluable comments on an earlier draft of this article.

Disclosure statement

No potential conflict of interest was reported by the author.

Funding

The work was supported by the Volkswagen Foundation [Az 93 273]

ORCID

Frieder R. Lang http://orcid.org/0000-0002-2660-1619

References

Bluck, S., & Alea, N. (2008). Remembering being me: the self-continuity function of autobiographical memory in younger and older adults. In F. Sani (Ed.), *Self Continuity: Individual and Collective Perspectives* (pp. 55–70). New York: Psychology Press.

Bühler, C. (1968). The course of human life as a psychological problem. *Human Development, 11* (3), 184–200. https://doi.org/10.1159/000270606

Carstensen, L. L., & Meeks, S. (2021). Socioemotional selectivity theory: The role of perceived endings in human motivation. *The Gerontologist, 61*(8), 1188–1196. https://doi.org/10.1093/geront/gnab116

Erikson, E. H. (1985). *The life cycle completed: A review.* Norton.

Hösch, H., Rupprecht, F. S., & Lang, F. R. (2023, in press). Psychological obsolescence and subjective remaining life expectancy are predictors of generativity in a six-year longitudinal study. *Journal of Adult Development.* https://doi.org/10.1007/s10804-023-09441-y

John, D., & Lang, F. R. (2015). Subjective acceleration of time experience in everyday life across adulthood. *Developmental Psychology, 51*(12), 1824–1839. https://doi.org/10.1037/dev0000059

Kaufmann, S. R. (1986). *The ageless self: Sources of meaning in late life*. University of Wisconsin Press.

Lang, F. R., & Carstensen, L. L. (2002). Time counts: Future time perspective, goals, and social relationships. *Psychology and Aging*, *17*(1), 125–139. https://doi.org/10.1037/0882-7974.17.1.125

Langer, E. J. (1992). Matters of mind: Mindfulness/mindlessness in perspective. *Consciousness and Cognition*, *1*(3), 289–305. https://doi.org/10.1016/1053-8100(92)90066-J

Langer, E. J. (2009). *Counterclockwise: Mindful health and the power of possibility*. Ballantine Books.

Lang, F. R., & Rupprecht, F. S. (2019). Motivation for longevity across the life span: An emerging issue. *Innovation in Aging*, *3*(2), 1–11. https://doi.org/10.1093/geroni/igz014

Lu, M., Li, A. Y., Fung, H. H., Rothermund, K., & Lang, F. R. (2018). Different future time perspectives interplay in predicting life satisfaction. *GeroPsych*, *31*(3), 103–113. https://doi.org/10.1024/1662-9647/a000192

Maslow, A. H. (1958). A dynamic theory of human motivation. In C. L. Stacey & M. DeMartino (Eds.), *Understanding human motivation* (pp. 26–47). Howard Allen Publishers. https://doi.org/10.1037/11305-004

Rank, O. (1996). Psychology and the soul. *Journal of Religion and Health*, *35*(3), 193–201. https://doi.org/10.1007/BF02354948

Tornstam, L. (2005). *Gerotranscendence: A developmental theory of positive aging*. Springer Publishing Company.

Wakefield, J. C. (1998). Immortality and the externalization of the self: Plato's unrecognized theory of generativity. In D. P. McAdams & E. de St. Aubin (Eds.), *Generativity and adult development* (pp. 133–174). APA.

Westphal, J. (2016). *The mind body problem*. MIT press.

Wikipedia. (2022), retrieved on Feb 14, 2023, https://en.wikipedia.org/wiki/Blind_men_and_an_elephant

Zimbardo, P., & Boyd, J. (2008). *The time paradox. The new psychology of time that will change your life*. Free Press.

Slower, deeper, wider: what soulful aging means to me

William L. Randall

ABSTRACT
Recently retired as a professor of gerontology, the author reflects on his own experience of aging. Drawing on the subfield of *narrative* gerontology, his area of specialization, and on age-related thoughts by writers like Florida Scott-Maxwell, Carl Jung, and Thomas Moore, he weaves together research concerning Gerotranscendence, Transpersonal Gerontology, and the transformative effects of so-called Near Death Experiences to articulate a vision of aging as, itself, a near-*ing* death experience. The result is a highly personal meditation on "soulful aging" as a matter of journeying slower, deeper, and wider into the intriguing landscape of later life.

Frankly, I hadn't even heard of "soulful aging" until invited to contribute to this special issue. As happens, though, when I encounter such enticing terms —"conscious aging," "creative aging," and "contemplative aging" also jump to mind, with each of which (for me at least) it overlaps in meaning – my brain went to work generating ideas that demanded jotting in my journal. I'm drawn to the phrase, in other words. It speaks to me, especially as I'm entering what feels like a fresh new chapter in my own life story: *The Third Chapter*, as Sarah Lawrence-Lightfoot (2009) calls it. Writing as a retiree, then, more than as a gerontologist, even a *narrative* one (though I'll say something on this soon enough), I'd like to explain why.

As for my retirement, it was a gradual process, thanks to the "package" that my university offered us pricey oldsters to tempt us out the door. Over a period of four years, I taught less and got paid less until, last summer, it was a done deal. So far it's been an intriguing transition. Things have been shifting and changing in curious ways. Not just my finances, but my priorities, my energies, my mind. It's as if I'm going slower, deeper, and wider all at once.

I'll let these three words guide me, then, as I ponder what "soulful aging" means to me.

Going slower

Two tumbles two years ago onto the same part of the same knee, plus the pain and the cane that, for a while, was part of daily life, forced me to realize how much – physically, at least – I was slowing down. It certainly made me think twice about putting in another year of mowing lawns, raking leaves, shoveling snow, and being on alert for the next darned thing in need of repair. Sometimes we say that such-and-such "brought me to my knees." Well, it was my knees that brought me to sell my house outside the city and, after 23 years, assume a simpler life in an apartment downtown. Fortunately, real estate was booming at the time and the transition went as well as it could. And, ironically (or was it more than irony at play?), despite two full months of decluttering and carting umpteen boxes of books (again!) from A to B, my knee emerged strangely refreshed. Having gotten me to move, it's nearly good as new.

At least where knees and hips are concerned, I've so far fared better than most. Biologists assure us, though, that slowing down comes naturally with age, both physically and neurologically, as with, for instance, increased "reaction time" in the transmission of information from eyes and ears to brains and limbs. I certainly don't subject my own limbs to jogging anymore; I take long strolls instead. Nor do I bound up the stairs two at a time like in the past. I pause on landings part-way up to catch my breath. But it's more of an internal kind of slowing that I'm hinting at here. It's slowing down so that I can step back, take the longer view of life, and attempt a bit to integrate myself – or more accurately, my *selves*: the several ones I've been across the years. It's straight out of Erik Erikson (1963): the urge that comes with age – though apparently not for all (Wink & Schiff, 2002)—to review our lives, to recall the key episodes and turning-points, positive and negative, and overall to pull ourselves together, figuratively speaking, till we attain some semblance of "ego integrity." In *The Measure of My Days*, a book I regularly return to for insights into what, for gerontology, has been the overlooked "inside" of later life, Florida Scott-Maxwell (1968), writing in her 80s, points to the prize to which our reviewing could lead: "When you truly possess all you have been and done," she says, "*which may take some time*," then "you are *fierce with reality*" (p. 42, emphasis mine). While I'm not sure how fierce with reality I'm likely to become, or what the phrase even means, I'll come back later to this type of internal slowing down. In the meantime, let me say that it's tied to an intellectual slowing too.

My slow-paced retirement has allowed time to morph into the sort of "slow professor" (Berg & Seeber, 2016) that I've always admired. I mean the kind who contemplates the larger, more delicious questions that there's scarcely time to ponder properly amid the bustle of academe, with all its prepping for lectures, competing for grants, and generally clambering up the ladder of scholarly achievement. I can sink into ideas in a more leisurely manner, allow my mind (which I've learned has a mind of its own!) to take its time circling around a given line of thought, not having to wrestle it to the mat beneath a pile of pretentious prose. With pen and paper handy while I take my daily walks, I scribble down whatever odd ideas bubble up from a brain that's more at rest.

Foremost among the slow questions that tug at me are those concerning a "narrative perspective" on life (Randall, 2001), on *later* life especially – a perspective that bridges the social sciences and humanities and that was seeded in me in my 20s as a student of theology. Those seeds grew to where I embarked upon a Ph.D. at Cambridge to delve into the autobiographical (read: narrative) dimensions of religious belief. As luck would have it, however, I dropped out of the program in under a year, not just for lack of funds, but for lack of focus, of preparation and maturity, to do justice to such a vast subject in an affordable span of time. When I went by his office to bid him goodbye, my tutor, seeking to assuage my sense of shame, offered the opinion that "it's often not until one's 40s that one acquires a point of view." Speaking from experience, and now as a *narrative* gerontologist, I've seen how true his words have turned out.

A narrative point of view needs time to ripen, time for ideas to cross-pollinate and sprout fresh ones in the corners of your mind. Because they reflect thinking within the humanities as much as the social sciences, such ideas can't be forced out in a programmatic manner and turned into "data" that can be shown on a chart or a graph. As my colleague, Gary Kenyon, and I have often said to one another, the views on biographical aging and on life-as-story that we've helped to advance will hopefully have a long shelf life. They've certainly had that for me, and they've evolved in some fascinating directions. To borrow a metaphor from James Birren, who pioneered a strategy for life review known as "guided autobiography", they've grown within me like a continually "branching tree" (Birren & Deutchman, 1991, p. 67).

My life's work – which has essentially been an unpacking of the "entailments" (Lakoff & Johnson, 1980) of the "root metaphor" (Sarbin, 1986) of "life as narrative" (Bruner, 1987)—has taken years to unfold, which in fact it's still doing. It's as if each presentation and publication has seen the shooting forth of yet another limb, or at least a twig or a leaf, and the fanning out of roots and sub-roots a little further into the composted remnants of books read and theories flirted with, not to mention seventy-odd years of Life, with the rich loam that all its losses and learnings, loves and selves, have laid down inside of me as, conceivably, my "soul" (see Randall, 2007). All the while, the central trunk – this stubborn hunch that we ARE, and not just HAVE, stories (Randall, 1995/2014), with all that it implies about the complexity and fluidity of "identity" over time – has been slowly but surely thickening in my mind.

Going deeper

When I was a minister, contemplating some passage of Scripture as I prepared for my Sunday sermon, I felt that I could never sink my teeth sufficiently into the themes it brought to mind. I had to move on to whatever texts the lectionary laid out for the following week, or gear up for the next high holy-day to which my message would need to be tailored. Plus, I had to keep my remarks comparatively uplifting lest I send my parishioners out the door more depressed than when they came in! This frustration is what drove me back to university at 38 to pursue my doctorate, publish my dissertation – a mother lode of ideas that, in fact, I continue to mine – and eventually become a tenured professor. At last, so I assumed, I could give full vent to my scholarly inclinations, could do more than skim the surface. While I was able to do so to a greater degree, there still didn't seem enough time to dig as deeply as I wanted, or as the themes in question deserved. But it's not just an intellectual deepening that I'm talking about. It's a personal one, an emotional one, and even, you might say, a psychic one.

Waking up these days later than I had to in the past, whether to dash off to a morning meeting or cram for an afternoon class, I can muse leisurely on what the night has brought. I can ponder the images and themes, the plotlines, and archetypes, that meandered through my dreams, or at least the few I'm capable of recalling. It's a luxury, no question, but not always an enjoyable one. I often find myself waking with an odd sort of knot in my stomach. I might have only the vaguest inkling of what it was I actually dreamed about, yet I feel unsettled for reasons I can't quite voice. Or I waken with my chest pounding, my most recent reverie, often seconds before I opened my eyes, revolving around some stressful scenario in which I'm racing to meet a deadline or catch a train or get up to speed as a pastor in a new community, a role which I know, deep down, will end up ruling my life. And my heart is racing too, although I'm never clear which racing causes which, nor is my cardiologist! Throughout my morning, then, I'm left wondering what currents are swirling in the depths? What "shadow stories" (de Medeiros & Rubinstein, 2015) should I be getting in touch with, and attempting to tell, if only to myself? What unlooked-at developmental business is Something or Someone nudging me to acknowledge? What existential issues, what spiritual questions, what shadowy sides of myself have I been evading that I finally need to face?

It seems, then, as if our psyche has its own slow questions, often life-long in nature. Carl Jung (1976) notes, for instance, that "the serious problems in life ... are never fully solved," that "the meaning and purpose of a problem seems to lie not in its solution but in our working at it incessantly" (p. 11). He also writes about how, amid "the afternoon of life," it is "a duty and necessity ... for the aging person ... to devote serious attention to himself" (p. 17), a duty to turn inward, as it were. Yet "the journey inward," observes Dag Hammerskjöld (1964), former Secretary-General of the United Nations and a closet mystic too, is "the longest journey" (p. 48). It's the longest, in part, because it's a journey without maps. While guidebooks abound to help us navigate our inner terrain, offering us templates for meditative practice, often in the company of others, it's a journey that we must ultimately make on our own. A journey which, despite critiques of Disengagement Theory, we may need to pull into a state of what I heard described once as "soulitude" to become acquainted with our inmost depths.

For me, that journey – and many of my dreamscapes reflect this – takes me into issues that I continue having around my father, a larger-than-life figure in my story, dead now for six years. By this I mean the lack of self-confidence that his irregular eruptions of anger – he, with his own shadows and insecurities – planted within me as a child. And I mean boundary issues, too: the power that I permitted his very presence, immediate or imagined, to have over my moods, my beliefs, and my relationships, especially intimate ones with women, those I almost married. From one night to another, my dreams can alternate between missing him acutely and being so angry with him that I want to kill him. And what about the dreams in which I'm back at university, sweating over an upcoming exam in a course I've barely attended, uncertain if I'll pass and, even more, what I'll do once (or whether) I get my degree, and generally feeling that there's some path I ought to be following but I haven't the foggiest idea what it is? When I waken and realize, to my great relief, that my career is safely behind me and that I've got all the degrees I'll ever need, I'm puzzled as to why my dream-self was so fretful, what it was trying to tell me. Is there something more – some higher goal or cause – that the universe is pushing me to pursue?

It's not just my dreams, though, that are luring me to go deeper. So, too, are my journals, plus all the other documents I've retained: letters that I wrote my parents during my university years and that my mother faithfully saved, letters that both of them, plus my sisters and other friends, including *girl*friends, wrote to me; to say nothing of files filled with notes and photos from assorted chapters in my story to date. Chalk it up to obsessive-compulsiveness, but mine is a well-chronicled life, or at least an *inner* life. Perhaps my innermost me has had me hold on to all of this stuff so that someday – i.e., now – I'll have time to pore properly over it and eventually "possess" it, as Scott-Maxwell says; to own it, or own *up* to it, all of it – the good, bad, and ugly, the things I'm proud of and those I'm not – and in this manner be "aging-in-depth" (Bianchi, 1991, p. 60); be *growing* old, as I'm fond of distinguishing, and not just getting old; be getting closer to my "true self" or the "real me", whatever such phrases might mean?

But pawing through old letters and photos, as committed as I am to doing it, is not necessarily the joyful jaunt down memory lane that one might wish. Rereading journals from my 20s and 30s (and even my 40s and 50s), I meet several of my former selves spewing out their half-baked thoughts and churned-up emotions, writhing on the page, selves I don't, in fact, especially like. They are "me's" I wish I hadn't been; guilt-ridden, God-haunted me's that are still beneath my father's sway. Put more charitably, they are me's I feel sorry for. I wish that I could reach out to them from their future, wrap my arms around them, and let them know that this too shall pass – whatever "this" might be, for typically my entries give no clue! I wish I could assure them that it's merely a chapter (or even a paragraph or page) in the ever-evolving narrative of their lives, however dark that passage might seem at the time; that brighter, lighter passages lie ahead; that the wider worldviews and larger selves which they'll eventually inhabit will welcome them, hang-ups and all, within the fold.

There's lots further that I want to—*need* to – go in this direction; for instance, in acknowledging facets of my nature that bear my father's stamp in more positive ways, and my mother's stamp as well, plus the stamp of my antecedents going back and back on either side, the stamp of the culture and era in which I was brought up, the communities and circumstances by which I've inevitably been shaped. And so on and so forth. But I find that I need to proceed at an intermittent pace. If I spend more than an hour or so at it, then I can slide into a mini-depression over missed opportunities, potentials not nurtured, relationships ended or abandoned, and therefore children not fathered and grandchildren not enjoyed. I can slip into a sadness that lingers for hours over the lost loves, lost selves, and unlived lives that (like everyone, no doubt) I inwardly lament. At such times, mired in regret, I take comfort, however, in the words of Thomas Moore (2017). In his book, *Ageless Soul*, he devotes a whole chapter to the theme of melancholy in later life, and our need to lean into it. "Feel the melancholy," he gently advises, "let it seep into [you], let it transform [you] into a genuine older person who is not always trying to make it otherwise" (p. 74). "In melancholy," he goes on, "you may discover things about yourself or your world that are not visible in a cheery atmosphere" (p. 76). . . . Melancholy can "*deepen your life*, give your perspective, and sharpen your understanding" (p. 80; emphasis mine).

For over four decades, the act of writing has been a key means of deepening my own life, through not just my journals but also the pages and pages of notes that I make when working on a given project, only a fraction of which worms its way into the final product. I can't understate how much I feel my inner life has been rendered more profound, or at least more complicated, by putting all these words onto the page. The writing life has very much been the reflective life, and the pace has only picked up. The more I write, the more I want to write *about*, and the better and deeper I want to write as well. More intensely by the day, I sense there's a wisdom within me and I'm keen to make out what it is (see Randall & Kenyon, 2001).

One book I keep revisiting is *At A Journal Workshop* by Jungian psychotherapist, Ira Progoff (1975). In it, he outlines a strategy for reviewing our lives known as "the intensive journal," one stage of which, for instance, is the "Inner Wisdom Dialogue" (pp. 269–284). Here are some of the alluring phrases he uses to capture what workshop participants tend to discover: "a connective thread [that] has been forming beneath the surface of our lives, carrying the meaning that has been trying to establish itself in our existence" (p. 11); "a process working at the depth of a person" (p. 27); "the personal depths that are unique to each individual [and] the *transpersonal* depth as well" (p. 79; emphasis mine); "the personal aspects of our lives lead beyond themselves and have implications for *the transpersonal meaning of our existence* as a whole" (p. 228, emphasis mine). Going ever deeper into the inner layers of our lives, such words suggest, is more than an exercise in self-absorption. Sooner or later, we come out the other side to where the personal and the universal converge.

Going wider

I've always been a voracious reader. But freed from the need to keep up with research in my field, my appetite has been extending in multiple directions. So many books, so little time: new books, books I've read but am keen to read again, and books I bought long, long ago but never read at all, more than likely because my brain wasn't ready for what they had to offer. The pile beside my favourite reading chair thus grows more varied by the week. I'm a kid in a candy shop, with a longing for learning like I've never really known. "Radical curiosity" (Dychtwald, 2021) concerning topics I'd at most only dabbled in has been unleashed. I go wherever it leads.

Glancing at that pile, I see books on everything from quantum physics to cosmotheology, and from narrative theory to near death experiences. I see biography, psychology, theology, paleontology, travel-writing, nature-writing, memoir, fiction, and *science* fiction too. I see books about the paranormal and life after life; about the secret life of birds and the hidden life of trees. Still just skimming the surface, you could argue, I graze from one to another and another, seldom consuming a volume from beginning to end, like I felt obliged to do as a paid academic, despite how boring or badly written it might be. In fact, my pace is quite slow, for even when reading a page-turner thriller, I'm always pausing to note things in my journal as countless threads of thought are sent spinning through my mind. My reading and writing lives are linked, each one fuelling the other in ways that keep me humble and excited alike. With very much a beginner's mind, I feel like I'm forever on the brink of some fresh synthesis of insight, as if these curiosities are calling me to weave them into a comprehensive worldview – or at least comprehensive for me, my own private (though open-ended) integration of "it all."

It's more than *ego* integrity after which I'm yearning, then. It's intellectual integrity. For one thing, as an inveterate narrativist, it's a yearning for a bigger story of *story* itself. In effect, my commitment to the study of story – which has been a core source of purpose in my life, what possibly I was put here to pursue, the "bliss" I've been fated to follow (Campbell & Moyers, 1988, p. 91) —has become the larger life that I strive to stay mindful of when the details of my day-to-day existence prove disheartening or dull. I'm thinking, for instance, of how my understanding of my own personal storyworld has been broadening of late from the essentially *horizontal*, or linear, approach to life-storywork that I've implicitly advocated – what's been called "big story narrative reflection" (Spector-Mersel, 2016)—towards the more *vertical*, or lyrical, approach that fellow narrative gerontologist, Oddgeir Synnes (2022, p. 51), sees as central to creative writing in later life, poetry-writing in particular (see Lehmann & Synnes, 2023). It's a process of "complex reminding" (Synnes et al., 2021) that I'm starting to engage in by exploring some of the more emotion-laden memories in my life, or even isolated moments—"small stories," as it were – and the meanings these may harbor, the questions that they raise. By throwing out an image or a metaphor to lasso a fleeting sentiment or idea (Randall, in press-a), I feel like I'm being opened out more than focussed in – as can happen when we seek to herd the events of our lives into a chronological, cause-and-effect, corral: *this happened, then this, then this.*

Better than prose perhaps, poetry can provide, therefore, a therapeutic function, can serve as "survival" (Orr, 2002). It can take us to rawer, fiercer places within ourselves; messier places, true, but airier and more honest ones as well, where our storyworlds can be opened out, making us inwardly richer and more resilient (Randall, 2013); where the currents of inner experience resist channeling into beginnings, middles, and ends; resist the restriction to which narrativization itself can sometimes lead; resist "narrative foreclosure" (Bohlmeijer et al., 2011). Aided by an increased capacity for "post-formal thought" that is said to come naturally with later life (Cohen, 2005, p. 36f)—a capacity that involves a greater openness to paradox and contradiction, ambiguity and irony – poetry-writing, as well as poetry-reading, can widen our inner worlds in ways that narrative prose may not and render later life truly "a time when entirely new perspectives on life can come forth" (Cohen, 2005, p. 83). Such widening, such "narrative openness" (Randall, 2013), is perhaps what Mark Freeman, with his career-long musings on "the poetics of selfhood" (Freeman, 1999), is pointing to in a passage that I often recite: "Our lives are like richly ambiguous texts to be interpreted and understood ... whose meanings are inexhaustible, whose mysterious existence ceaselessly calls forth the desire to know, whose readings cannot ever yield a final closure" (Freeman, 1993, p. 184).

Again, it's more than an intellectual widening that I want to talk about here. It's a spiritual one as well. I want to widen not merely my personal "horizon of self-understanding" (Berman, 1994, p. 180). And I want to widen not just my horizon of understanding on the world of narrative ideas, as passionate as I have been about promoting them in my teaching and writing and in the conferences I've helped put on—endeavours which, taken together, I think of as "the bigger story" of my life. In fact, I've taped a typed mantra to my refrigerator door to help me keep things in perspective when I'm feeling lost or alone: *Stay Rooted In The Big Story of Your Life*. But beyond all of this, I want to expand my horizon on the world as a whole.

Many have described aging as a "spiritualizing" process (Wacks, 2011, p. 128), not necessarily religion-izing, but spiritualizing, which has broader connotations. A former minister of religion, I find myself spiraling back therefore to convictions that were once my stock in trade. But it's not like I'm returning to them full circle, for I'm not in the same place anymore, whether professionally or personally. My world feels wider in scope, not nearly as parochial as it was in the past by virtue of my vocation and my youth. In my preaching and counselling (such as it was), my duty at the time, I believed, was to provide my parishioners with answers more than questions, certainties not ambiguities. With both – questions and ambiguities – I've grown more comfortable, however, partly because of post-formal thinking and partly because I experience my life to be unfolding, more palpably almost, within a vaster context. Passages like these by psychologist, Adrian Van Kaam (1972) —whose works I first encountered as a rookie cleric under the big sky of Saskatchewan – resonate with me in more immediate ways: "Feeling rooted in something that surpasses all events," he writes, "I am no longer overwhelmed by the happenings around me. I can see beyond them. I can locate them against a wider horizon" (p. 30f) "No convictions," he says, "are of a wider scope and power than spiritual convictions. They offer an eternal perspective, an infinite horizon" (Van Kaam, 1974, p. 114).

It's this infinite horizon after which, in my reading and writing, my thinking and living, I'm hankering all the more. It's what Freeman may also have in mind when he refers to "the theological moment of the life story" (Freeman, 2018) and to "the *transcendent horizon* of the life story" (2010, p. 94, emphasis Freeman's). It's a horizon toward which many feel pulled, for instance, as they engage in genealogical research, in tracing the roots of their families, like my father loved doing in fact, only it's on a grander scale. It's implicit, too, in a modest but intriguing body of thinking known as "transpersonal gerontology" (see, e.g., Wacks, 2011). And it is the very open-endedness of this horizon, its infinity, to which I find myself most drawn. Yet the widening I'm getting at concerns the heart as much as the mind.

Uncle Winston, my mother's oldest brother, was born with a condition described at the time as "an enlarged heart," the formal, medical term being *cardiomegaly*. In tandem with this, lucky lad that he was, he had major developmental and mobility issues too. I imagine kids in on the playground taunting him as "retarded." As a kid myself, visiting the village in Nova Scotia where he lived with my grandparents, I found him quite scary. With his twisted body, his crab-like way of walking, and his distorted almost howling voice, there was scant chance of carrying on an ordinary conversation. Looking back, I have no idea what his thoughts might have been, including his thoughts about me, no idea what it was like for him to BE him. Dead at 52, he was an enigma to me. And so too, you could say, is my mother, though for sweeter reasons.

Every evening when she gets into bed at the facility where she resides, she picks up her phone and starts dialing various people in her circle, as many as 30 per night (over 100 are on her list in total), all of them younger than she is, many by a longshot. And she knows all of their numbers by heart. She calls them, though, not to complain about *her* situation – living in a nursing home, all but blind due to macular degeneration, unable to move about without a walker, and needing assistance when she goes to the toilet – but to ask them about theirs: "Will your daughter make it home for the holidays? Did the doctor get back to you about the tests you had done?". And so on and so forth. And she ends each call by telling them "I love you very much." Like her brother, her heart, too, has seriously enlarged, though in life-enhancing, not life-threatening, ways. I like to think that my own heart is doing the same. While I have miles to go in order to match her record, I'm blessed at present with a circle of friends of various ages (not something that many men my age apparently possess), each of whom enriches my life and stretches my horizons in distinctive directions.

As I write this, Mother has just entered her 102nd year. She's clearly in the realm of "deep old age" (de Lange, 2015, p. viii), a point that leads me to venture one last thought on going wider. Living this long, she is closing in, no question, on the proverbial Final Frontier. She's in the midst of – and aging in general, I propose, can be seen as – a Near-*ing* Death Experience, or an NDE, with similar sorts of effects – emotionally and psychologically – that NDEr's report when they return from "the other side" (Pike, 1968); an experience that opens "windows into a more comprehensive picture of the world" (Greyson, 2021; see also Lommel, 2007; Moody, 2012). Besides the panoramic life review that it commonly involves, the effects to which NDEr's attest include a lessened attachment to material possessions, a heightened hunger for learning, an enhanced sense of meaning and purpose, a deepened appreciation for the sanctity of life and the power of love, a nostalgia for their real "home"—a reality that they found realer (and fiercer?) than this one – and, above all, a dramatic reduction in their fear of death. "Death is not the end," is the feeling they report in their re-born frame of mind, but simply "a horizon past which the five senses cannot see" (Robbins & Mortifee, 1991, p. 77). Susan McFadden and Robert Atchley echo such a sentiment in saying that aging and "the encounter with temporality"—or with our "finitude" (Baars, 2010)—"shift our gaze toward *the horizon of mystery*" (McFadden & Atchley, 2001, p. xiii; emphasis mine). I find this perspective incredibly enticing, but more than this, essential to incorporate into our day-to-day awareness. For I agree with those who claim that we need a "cosmology of death" (Schlitz et al., 2011), a vision of death and aging alike that ushers discussions of them out of a biomedical context and situates them within that of our ever-expanding understanding of the universe itself, in all its vastness, open-ness, and multidimensionality (Randall, 2020).

Bearing this in mind, and given the odd sorts of books to which I tend to be drawn, I'd like to propose here that we view nearing The End as analogous to a rocket ship, its earlier stages long since jettisoned, approaching an enormous black hole at nearly the speed of light. As our vessel enters the "event horizon," we, its occupants, will experience time differently than the folks back home, assuming they're still alive! Its passage will slow and slow until it seems to stop altogether, as it's been argued happens for the dying person[1] and which Lars Tornstam (1996), with his theory of "gerotranscendence," posits comes naturally with very late life. Not only do the boundaries between Self and Other tend to blur, as well as those between Life and Death, but Past and Future (distinctions so taken-for-granted yet, from a quantum perspective, so arbitrary too) merge more into the Now of "one day at a time"—as I feel they are for Mother! It's as if she's living in a different type of time—"kairos time" versus "chronos time," some might say – and has morphed into what one care provider to nursing home residents affectionately refers to as "Advent people" (McFadden & Thibault, 2001, p. 241).

Meanwhile, back at the black hole ... Provided our vehicle's trajectory toward the dark, spinning giant is calibrated correctly, we're eventually thrust out the other side – perhaps through a network of wormholes – into a whole different region of space-time, if not a different universe entirely, both "elsewhere" and "elsewhen" (Gribbin, 1979, p. 75f).

Though some might deem this a silly analogy (actually, it figured pivotally in the movie made from Carl Sagan's novel *Contact*, and several edge-of-the-edge scientists accept its possibility)—it fills me with wonder, the sort of "what if?" spirit that I feel we need far more of in gerontology, a field critiqued for being "rich in data but poor in theory" (Birren & Bengston, 1988, p. ix). It's the very sort of wonder which Scott-Maxwell (1968) was likely experiencing when she penned these words in her journal: "All is uncharted and uncertain," she writes; "we [older people] seem to lead the way into the unknown" (p. 139). After noting that "It has taken me all the time I've had to become myself," she admits that, paradoxically, "now that I am old there are times when I feel I am barely here, no room for me at all." She goes on: "I remember that in the last months of my pregnancies the child seemed to claim almost all my body, my strength, my breath, and I held on wondering if my burden was my enemy, uncertain as to whether my life was at all mine. *Is life a pregnancy?*", she asks rhetorically. "*That would make death a birth*? (p. 76; emphasis mine). If Scott-Maxwell is onto something beyond mere wishful thinking, then it hints that our whole narrative of aging, its meaning and end, might need a radical turning around. If, as the poet says, "in our end is our beginning," which coincidentally most of the world's main spiritual traditions have proposed all along, then possibly we've gotten the story backward?

A few further considerations

My thoughts here on going slower, deeper, and wider are but first forays, of course, into a topic to which I'd given no conscious consideration until asked to write this piece. They're hardly presented, then, as a recipe for soulful aging, or what it should be for others. I've written out of my personal experience alone. I've written out of the belief that gerontology is one of those subjects that sooner or later we become more interested in whether we want to or not, which is why I've found it difficult during my career to keep myself out of my inquiries and remain "objective" and "unbiased." As an unrepentant "narrative inquirer" (Clandinin, 2007) it has proven impossible to keep myself out of the equation. Research, for me, has always been *in*-search too. My point is that as a white, Western, well-educated male, with an introspective, dilettantish bent (and thus far without dementia or other major disability), my views on anything are scarcely universal. All I can do is tell my own story, or at least my story at this stage. Ask me to write on the same topic when I'm in "the fourth chapter" or the fifth and I'll likely tell a different tale. In the meantime, I have homework that I need to do; indeed, that we all have to do. There is important business to be getting on with, in other words, if we would shift from being just *older* to being *Elder*: "philosophic homework," it's been described as (Randall, 2022; Schacter-Shalomi & Miller, 1995, pp. 124–127). In my own case, this means not just reading and writing as much as I can, but – following my mother's lead – opening my heart and mind as widely as possible, learning whatever and however I am able. I want to be ready . . .

Over the years, I've become a respecter of synchronicities (see Bolen, 1979; Peat, 1987; Storm, 2008). In my näivete, perhaps, I think of them as nudges from beyond – my knee's recovery as an example?—or as "signs" that whatever else is happening in my life, things are unfolding as they must, that nothing is totally an accident. Amid the comings and goings of my otherwise ordinary life, I often sense this strange connectedness at work, especially in times of significant personal transition. Bumping into this individual on this exact day? Why!? Getting into a conversation on just this topic at just this juncture?

What's going on!? Receiving a request to speak or write on just this theme at just this stage? It seems so meant-to-be. These sorts of invitations show up, I've found, when my mind or soul (a term I've intentionally not defined) has suitably evolved – has deepened and widened – to where I might actually have something worthy to contribute to the discussion, not to mention something I myself can learn, that I *need* to learn. In this case, though, the contribution hasn't been hammered out in confident, formulaic fashion. It is offered humbly, tentatively. It is an attempt (literally: an *essai*) to add a strand to the discussion that might not otherwise be woven in. Worthy or not, working on it has itself felt uncannily timed in terms of my own development – intellectual, emotional, and spiritual. *When the writer is ready, the right project will arrive.*

Naturally, there's much more to life than writing. Yet rightly or wrongly, it's been an enormous part of my own. I agree with the view, therefore, that "writing is, essentially, an act of discovery" (Wahlstrom, 2006, p. 65): discovery of the subject that you're writing about, discovery of how intricate it actually is, and discovery of yourself. It is a means of "autobiographical learning" (Randall, 2010), in other words, learning about yourself and *from* yourself, from your own story. As I say, the more I write, the deeper and wider I want to go, my world, both inner and outer, feeling limitless in scope. At the same time, I'm quietly embarrassed that this has been the case. And I can occasionally wallow in self-pity at how, alongside of others my age, notably other men, I've consumed so much of my time in fussing over ideas, at best ephemeral things, rather than "giving back" to society in more tangible, acceptable ways.

At such times, though, I console myself with the thought that my publications themselves have, in a sense, been my children. What I've lacked by way of biological or parental "generativity", a lack I clearly regret, I like to think that I've made up for, at least a little, in intellectual productivity, in "spreading the word" - about *Narrative*, for example. And I've certainly, parent-like, poured lots of myself (some might say too much) into what I've written, launching each of my offspring into the big wide world where, with any luck at all, they'll find their way to ready readers whose thoughts will hopefully be enriched. Like my own have been by writers such as Teilhard de Chardin (1960) . . .

Equal parts paleontologist and priest, scientist and mystic, Chardin speaks of "the hidden mystery in the womb of death" (p. 107), a phrase that I intend to make central to my personal *ars moriendi* creed. As hinted at by Scott-Maxwell, with her thoughts on death as birth, as transition instead of termination, our allotted life-time may – who knows?—be but one chapter in a far longer narrative of the Self, in which case, not finitude but IN-finitude may be the operative feature of human existence. I'm certainly not alone in imagining this possibility (see Greyson, 2021; Lommel, 2007; Moody, 2012), although few gerontologists have publicly entertained it. But one passage especially by Chardin never fails to raise my sights to the "infinite horizon" that I mentioned before. It points to a synthesis of science and spirituality, to a "cosmotheology" (Dick, 2000), that is long overdue. Having made it central to my own morning meditation, let me include it to help "conclude" my musings here:

> Every force which moves through me, envelops me, or captivates me emanates from the divine will as its fundamental source ... Thus every contact, whether it caresses me, pierces me, bruises me, jostles me ... or crushes me, is a contact with one of the forms, multiple but in every case adorable, of the hand of God. God, too, is the source of all the elements of which I am composed.... God is vibrant in the ether; and through it he [sic.] penetrates to the very marrow of my material being. By the ether all material bodies are joined, influence one another, and support one another in the unity of the vast sphere whose ultimate boundary we cannot even imagine. (Cuénot, 1965, p. 36f).

It's no accident that this essay itself reads a little like a story. In the beginning, you are ushered slowly into storytime; in the middle, taken deeper into the "trouble" that any story requires for it to work (Bruner, 1999, p. 8); and in the end brought out, like Chardin's words may do, into a wider, happy-ever-after world where "thou, my soul, at length are free," as the poet exults, "leaving thine outgrown shell by life's unresting sea" (Holmes, 2015/1895). Prevailing views on aging in our modern society – not to mention in gerontology itself, which continues to be dominated by a materialist-reductionist paradigm – go sharply, of course, against this Pollyanna storyline. According to those views, which implicitly presume a universe with no intrinsic meaning or purpose, aging is little more than a sad saga of disability and decline that leads unswervingly to death. Apart from this, there is no cosmic consciousness within which Everything – black holes, wormholes, oak trees, monkeys, molecules, and dreams – is bound together by "the ether," by an underlying wholeness or "implicate order" (Bohm, 1980), an "undulating quantum foam" (Koestler, cited in Grant, 1985, p. 307) or quantum field that is seething with potential. Rather, there is ... Nothing at all.

For years, I've been aching to articulate a counter-story to this bleak "narrative of decline" (Gullette, 2004). I've been wanting to "re-genre-ate" aging from the unmitigated tragedy that, deep down, many experience it as being, to more of an *adventure*: a journey into the unknown, into Mystery, a stage therefore of deep learning, even awe, the fulfillment of the life-cycle, arguably, and not merely its depressing denouement (Nouwen & Gaffney, 1976). Indeed, writing on "age as adventure" is my next main project (see Randall, in press-b), for which Scott-Maxwell (1968) is again my inspiration: "I want to tell people approaching and perhaps fearing age," she writes, "that it is a time of discovery. If they say— 'of what?' I can only answer, 'We must each find out for ourselves, otherwise it won't be discovery'" (p. 142).

Going slower, deeper, and wider, with a quiet openness to what wonders might lie in wait: this is central, I've learned from writing this, to what "soulful aging" means to me.

Note

1. "At the moment that death becomes unavoidable, chemicals are released into the brain . . . chemicals . . . virtually identical to those released during an epileptic seizure . . . [P]sychological time begins to slow down for the dying person. In effect, they fall out of the time perspective of any observers who may be witnessing the death" (Peake, 2010, p. 369f).

Disclosure statement

No potential conflict of interest was reported by the author.

References

Baars, J. (2010). Philosophy of aging, time, and finitude. In T. Cole, R. Ray, & R. Kastenbaum (Eds.), *A guide to humanistic studies in aging* (pp. 105–120). The Johns Hopkins University Press.

Berg, M., & Seeber, B. (2016). *The slow professor: Changing the culture of speed in the academy*. University of Toronto Press.

Berman, H. (1994). *Interpreting the aging self: Personal journals of later life*. Springer.

Bianchi, E. (1991). A spirituality of aging. In L. Cahill & D. Mieth (Eds.), *Aging* (pp. 58–64). SCM Press.

Birren, J., & Bengston, V. (Eds.). (1988). *Emergent theories of aging*. Springer.

Birren, J., & Deutchman, D. (1991). *Guiding autobiography groups for older adults: Exploring the fabric of life*. The Johns Hopkins University Press.

Bohlmeijer, E., Westerhof, G., Randall, W., Tromp, T., & Kenyon, G. (2011). Narrative foreclosure: Preliminary considerations for a new sensitizing concept. *Journal of Aging Studies*, *25*(4), 364–370. https://doi.org/10.1016/j.jaging.2011.01.003

Bohm, D. (1980). *Wholeness and the implicate order*. Routledge.

Bolen, J. (1979). *The Tao of psychology: Synchronicity and the self*. Harper & Row.

Bruner, J. (1987). Life as narrative. *Social Research*, *5*(4), 1).11–32.

Bruner, J. (1999). Narratives of aging. *Journal of Aging Studies*, *13*(1), 7–9. https://doi.org/10.1016/S0890-40659980002-4

Butler, R. (1963). The life review: An interpretation of reminiscence in the aged. *Psychiatry*, *26*(1), 65–76. https://doi.org/10.1080/00332747.1963.11023339

Campbell, J., & Moyers, B. (1988). *The power of myth*. Doubleday.

Clandinin, J. (Ed.). (2007). *Handbook of narrative inquiry: Mapping a methodology*. Sage.

Cohen, G. (2005). *The mature mind: The positive power of aging brain*. Basic Books.

Cuénot, C. (1965). *Teilhard de Chardin: A biographical study*. (V. Colimore), Ed.). Helicon.

de Lange, F. (2015). *Loving later life: An ethics of aging*. Eerdmans.

de Medeiros, K., & Rubinstein, R. (2015). "Shadow stories" in oral interviews: Narrative care through careful listening. *Journal of Aging Studies*, *34*, 162–168. https://doi.org/10.1016/j.jaging.2015.02.009

Dick, S. (2000). Cosmotheology: Theological implications of the new universe. In S. Dick (Ed.), *Many worlds: The new universe, extraterrestrial life, & the theological implications* (pp. 191–210). Templeton Foundation Press.

Dychtwald, K. (2021). *Radical curiosity: One man's purpose for cosmic magic and a purposeful life*. Unnamed Press.

Erikson, E. (1963). *Childhood and society* (2nd ed.). W. W. Norton.

Freeman, M. (1993). *Rewriting the self: History, memory, narrative.* Routledge.

Freeman, M. (1999). Life narratives, the poetics of selfhood, and the redefinition of psychological theory. In W. Maiers, B. Bayer, B. Esgalhado, R. Jorna, & E. Schraube (Eds.), *Challenges to theoretical psychology* (pp. 245–250). Captus.

Freeman, M. (2018). Commentary: The theological moment of the life story. *Journal of Theoretical and Philosophical Psychology, 38*(2), 107–115. https://doi.org/10.1037/teo0000089

Grant, P. (Ed.). (1985). *A dazzling darkness: An anthology of western mysticism.* Collins.

Greyson, B. (2021). *After: A doctor explores what near-death experiences reveal about life and beyond.* St. Martins Essentials.

Gribbin, J. (1979). *Timewarps.* Sphere Books.

Gullette, M. (2004). *Aged by culture.* University of Chicago Press.

Hammerskjöld, D. (1964). *Markings.* (I. Sjöberg & W. Auden, Eds.). Ballantine.

Holmes, O. (2015/1895). The chambered nautilus. *The poetical works of oliver wendell holmes.* Andesite Press.

Jung, C. G. (1976). The stages of life. In J. Campbell (Ed.), *The portable Jung* (pp. 3–22). Penguin.

Lakoff, G., & Johnson, M. (1980). *Metaphors we live by.* University of Chicago Press.

Lawrence-Lightfoot, S. (2009). *The third chapter: Passion, risk, and adventure in the 20 years after 50.* Sarah Crichton Books.

Lehmann, O., & Synnes, O. (Eds.). (2023). *A poetic language of ageing.* Bloomsbury Academic.

Lommel, P. (2007). *Consciousness beyond life: The science of the near-death experience.* HarperPerrenial.

McFadden, S., & Atchley, R. (Eds.). (2001). *Aging and the meaning of time: A multidisciplinary exploration.* Springer.

McFadden, S., & Thibault, J. (2001). *Chronos* to *kairos*: Christian perspectives on time and aging. In S. McFadden & R. Atchley (Eds.), *Aging and the meaning of time* (pp. 229–250). Springer.

Moody, R. (2012). *Paranormal: My life in pursuit of the afterlife.* HarperOne.

Moore, T. (2017). *Ageless soul: The lifelong journey toward meaning and joy.* St. Martin's.

Nouwen, H., & Gaffney, W. (1976). *Aging: The fulfillment of life.* Anchor.

Orr, G. (2002). *Poetry as survival.* The University of Georgia Press.

Peake, A. (2010). *Is there life after death? The extraordinary science of what happens when we die.* Arcturus.

Peat, D. (1987). *Synchronicity: The bridge between matter and mind.* Bantam.

Pike, J. (1968). *The other side: My experiences with psychic phenomena.* Dell.

Progoff, I. (1975). *At a journal workshop: The basic text and guide for using the intensive journal.* Dialogue House Library.

Randall, W. (in press-b). Age as adventure: Restorying later life. *Narrative Works: Issues, Investigations, and Interventions.*

Randall, W. (in press-a). The poetics of growing old: Metaphoric competence and the philosophic homework of later life. In O. Lehmann & O. Synnes (Eds.), *A poetic language of aging.* Bloomsbury.

Randall, W. (1995/2014). *The stories we are: An essay on self-creation* (2nd ed.). University of Toronto Press.

Randall, W. (2001). Storied worlds: Acquiring a narrative perspective on aging, identity, and everyday life. In G. Kenyon, P. Clark, & B. de Vries (Eds.), *Narrative gerontology: Theory, research, and practice* (pp. 31–62). Springer.

Randall, W. (2007). From computer to compost: Rethinking our metaphors for memory. *Theory & Psychology, 17*(5), 611–633. https://doi.org/10.1177/0959354307081619

Randall, W. (2010). Storywork: Autobiographical learning in later life. In C. Clark & M. Rossiter (Eds.), *Narrative perspectives on adult education: New directions for adult and continuing education, 126* (pp. 25–36). Jossey-Bass.

Randall, W. (2013). The importance of being ironic: Narrative openness and personal resilience in later life. *The Gerontologist, 53*(1), 9–16. https://doi.org/10.1093/geront/gns048

Randall, W. (2020). The end of the story? Narrative openness in life and death. *Narrative Works: Issues, Investigations, and Interventions, 9*(2), 152–170. https://doi.org/10.7202/1076530ar

Randall, W. (2022). The philosophic homework of later life: On narrative, wisdom, and the positive potential of growing old. In A. Teodorescu & D. Chiribucă (Eds.), *Shaping ageing: Social transformations and enduring meanings* (pp. 13–26). Routledge.

Randall, W., & Kenyon, G. (2001). *Ordinary wisdom: Biographical aging and the journey of life*. Praeger.

Robbins, J., & Mortifee, A. (1991). *In search of balance: Discovering harmony in a changing world*. H. J. Kramer.

Sarbin, T. (1986). The narrative as a root metaphor for psychology. In T. Sarbin (Ed.), *Narrative psychology: The storied nature of human conduct* (pp. 3–21). Praeger.

Schacter-Shalomi, Z., & Miller, R. (1995). *From age-ing to sage-ing: A profound new vision of growing older*. Warner.

Schlitz, M., Vieten, C., & Erickson-Freeman, K. (2011). Conscious aging and worldview transformation. *The Journal of Transpersonal Psychology, 43*(2), 223–238.

Scott-Maxwell, F. (1968). *The measure of my days*. Penguin.

Spector-Mersel, G. (2016). Life story reflection in social work education: A practical model. *Journal of Social Work Education, 53*(2), 286–299. https://doi.org/10.1080/10437797.2016.1243498

Storm, L. (Ed.). (2008). *Synchronicity: Multiple perspectives on meaningful coincidence*. Pari Publishing.

Synnes, O. (2022). A tune beyond us, yet ourselves": An ethics of the unconscious and cultural citizenship in dementia. In K. Fjetland, A. Gjermestad, & I. Lid (Eds.), *Lived citizenship for persons in vulnerable life situations: Theories and practices* (pp. 46–62). Scandinavian University Press.

Synnes, O., Raheim, M., Lykkeslet, E., & Gjengedal, E. (2021). A complex reminding: The ethics of poetry writing in dementia care. *Dementia, 20*(3), 1025–1043. https://doi.org/10.1177/1471301220922750

Teilhard de Chardin, P. (1960). *Le Milieu divin : An essay on the interior life*. Fontana.

Tornstam, L. (1996). Gerotranscendence: A theory about maturing into old age. *Journal of Aging and Identity, 1*(1), 37–49.

Van Kaam, A. (1972). *On being yourself: Reflections on spirituality and originality*. Dimension Books.

Van Kaam, A. (1974). *Spirituality and the gentle life*. Dimension Books.

Wacks, V. Q. (2011). The elder as sage, old age as spiritual path: Towards a transpersonal gerontology. *The Journal of Transpersonal Psychology, 43*(2), 127–155.

Wahlstrom, R. (2006). *The Tao of writing: Imagine, create, flow*. Adams Media.
Wink, P., & Schiff, B. (2002). To review or not to review? The role of personality and life events in life review and adaptation to older age. In J. Webster & B. Haight (Eds.), *Critical advances in reminiscence: From theory to application* (pp. 44–60). Springer.

The Jewish soulful aging of Jacques Élie Derrida

Stephen Katz

ABSTRACT

The essay explores the Jewish life and career of Jacques Derrida (1930–2004), suggesting how, with age, his understanding of his destiny as leader of a transformative intellectual movement grew into a soulful journey. Derrida's celebrated volume of work, based on his masterful concept of deconstruction, is seen as integral to his personal struggle with his Jewishness. While Derrida has been the subject of numerous biographies, including many that debate the influence of his Jewish background, this essay considers more directly how his quest to discover alternative spaces of language and thought (and refuge) became increasingly linked to his interpretations of the radicality of Judaic traditions. The argument moves from a discussion of his childhood as an Algerian Sephardic Jew to his career and life in Paris, to the relationship between deconstruction and spirituality, and finally, to his reckoning in his later years with survivorship, legacy, faith, and wisdom as guides to his internal desert of wandering and revelation.

Jacques Élie Derrida (1930–2004) was one of the most famous philosophers of the postwar era, best known for his complex and inventive critiques of the major thinkers and intellectual movements of modern European thought. Positioning himself within the heady debates between Marxists, humanists, structuralists, poststructualists, and phenomenologists, Derrida charted new interpretations of the works of Claude Lévi-Strauss, Edmund Husserl, Georg Wilhelm Friedrich Hegel, Michel Foucault, Friedrich Nietzsche, Martin Heidegger, and Søren Kierkegaard, among many others, including literary and artistic figures. His body of the literature and that which grew around him was voluminous and tremendously influential not only within academic spheres but also in reframing their foundations and conventions, as ubiquitous Derridean terms, such as "grammatology," "logocentricism," "deconstruction," "différance," "the trace," and "metaphysics of presence" articulated new vocabularies of inquiry, debate, and textuality. In particular, Derrida's philosophy of deconstruction grew into an adventurous style of thought that traveled outside of France, unsettling wherever it took hold to embolden a generation of global scholars pursuing alterity and justice to contest disciplinary traditions and authorities (for example, at Yale University). As with his contemporaries, such as Michel Foucault and Roland Barthes, Derrida became a celebrated media star, attracting large crowds at conferences and public lectures, appearing in televised interviews and documentary films (e.g., *Derrida* (2002)), with each event spinning out further reviews and discussions about the status of his work and the dilemmas of philosophy in modern society.

While the terrain of Derrida's work begins with the legacy of Plato, his *life* as a philosopher, beyond his popularity and scholarship, holds a different importance, one which this essay aims to explore. In particular, I am interested in Derrida's Jewishness. While many Derrida experts have written about his Jewishness, whether as part of his biographical background or as a critical resource with which to counter Christian and 'Greek' discourses of truth (as elaborated below), I am curious about another set of intersections that cross between Derrida's Jewishness, his philosophical approaches, his aging, and his soulfulness. And by soulfulness, I am thinking about that space of interiority, the "inside" of our aging that grows and folds against the permutations, risks, and opportunities of the "outside," but that gains in spiritual dynamism, presence, insight, and fulfillment with age. I wish to argue that in Derrida's later years, it was this soulfulness that heightened his sense of reflexivity, compassion, and humility about what he had accomplished and why, and created an expansive awareness for him as to how and why his Jewishness had been a guide in the wilderness of his adopted country and culture (France), and even how the meaning of deconstruction itself resonated with a spiritual brilliance deeply rooted in the Jewish search for a God-based enlightenment. In a word, I wish to propose that the many "outsides" Derrida sought to occupy, the margins he embraced, and the absences and silences he gave voice to with his writing, eventually came to rest within his own internalized desert, a space of wandering, clarity, and soulful discovery. As such, this essay is less concerned with the periods, stages, and turns of Derrida's thinking, than with the non-linear but gradual accumulation of reckoning with the spiritual dimension of his Jewishness.

The life of thought and spirit

There is no shortage of writing about the fascinating twists and turns by which lives, contexts, and ideas, and I would add souls too, have come together to create and shape our scholarly communities. In anthropology, Clifford Geertz's *Works and Lives: The Anthropologist as Author* (Geertz, 1988) is a wonderful documentation of how anthropologists have written and invested themselves in their research, often without knowing it. Likewise, Berkeley anthropologist Paul Rabinow wrote in *Making PCR [Polymerase Chain Reaction]: The Story of Biotechnology* Rabinow (1996) about how scientists and their findings were conjoined in the development of the human genome project. The field of urban sociology developed with Georg Simmel and Louis Wirth because they both lived in large cities; Simmel lived in Berlin, the largest metropolis in Europe in the early twentieth century, when he wrote 'The metropolis and mental life' in 1903 (Simmel, 1971); and Wirth lived in bustling, multicultural, and agonistic Chicago when he wrote 'Urbanism as a way of life' in 1938 (Wirth, 1938). However, in many of these illustrious careers a soulful dimension is often concealed, emerging in unpredictable and inspiring ways. For example, for Simmel (banned from teaching at the University of Berlin because he was Jewish), underpinning his seminal sociological studies of fashion, the arts, the senses, leisure, and consumerism was a vision of universal harmony that expressed the transcendent nature of human sociality:

> The essence of aesthetic observation and interpretation lies in the fact that the typical is to be found in what is unique, the lawlike in what is fortuitous, the essence and significance of things in the superficial and transitory .... To the adequately trained eye, the total beauty, the total meaning of the world as a whole radiates from every single point. (Simmel in Frisby, 1992, p. 18)

Another telling and touching example is the evolutionary scientist Loren Eiseley (1907–1977), who was as much of a poet as he was a scientist, and who produced models of the universe with soulful reverence and naturalistic wonder. Vivian Gornick, in her book *The Men in My Life* (Gornick, 2008), talks about Eiseley's life and his ideas. Born in the open country of Nebraska to a very poor family, Eiseley's mother was deaf and his father died young. He dropped out of school at the age of 19 to wander alone across the country during the Depression, returning to school in the 1920s. While the young Eiseley lived much of his life alone, Gornick says that "within himself, the boy turned away to the glorious emptiness before him, to the birds and [other] animals, the fossils and desert striations to be found out on the sub-baked Nebraska plain. Here, in *this* silence, he did not feel alone" (p. 56, emphasis original). This sense of divine isolation inhabits Eiseley's writing, beginning very obviously with his first book, *The Immense Journey* (Eiseley, 1957).

In the spirit of Simmel, Eiseley, and many others, I wish to consider Derrida's life from a soulful vantage point, which begins at the site of his birth as a Sephardic Jew, in El Biar, Algeria, July 15, 1930. It was there and then, according to Derrida, that his circumcision (referred to by the French as a "baptism") marked him as an individual, but with a covenant to God that entailed ensuing lifelong conflicts of belonging. While Derrida's real (Jewish) name was Élie, his parents, attempting to be more modern (and American), called him Jackie, after Hollywood movie actor Jackie Coogan. Growing up in a Muslim Arabic country under French colonial rule, meant that Derrida experienced various forms of anti-Semitism, the worst of which occurred during the war years where, under the influence of the Vichy government, strict quotas for Jewish students were introduced in public schools. Derrida, at age 12, was stripped of his French nationality and could only attend a Jewish school (see Peeters, 2012; Salmon, 2020). Thus, he says that the word "Jew" for him was already laden with the meaning of "a denial of right rather than the right to belong to a legitimate group" (Derrida, 2007b, p. 10); further, he wonders if his becoming skilled at interpreting, his "trained vigilance," began with his experiencing and recognizing anti-Semitism and his undergoing an "interrupted belonging" stemming from both the anti-Semitic colonial Algerian regime, and the restrictive traditions of his own Jewish community (Derrida, 2007b, p. 15), as I elaborate below.

Derrida (now Jacques) moved to Paris in 1949, was admitted to École Normale Supérieure (ENS) in 1952, where be began his stellar rise in philosophy, graduating through the various levels, exams, and publications required of him, until getting a permanent position at ENS. But it was during the 1960s when Derrida emerged as a brilliant literary and theoretical figure, publishing his three ground-breaking books in 1967, *Writing and Difference, Speech and Phenomena*, and *Of Grammatology*. Derrida was offered a number of visiting positions, which he took up with particular influence at several major American campuses, and, in time, received multiple honorary doctorates and awards around the world. Stunned by his masterful challenges to philosophical traditions – ontology, ethics, linguistics, hermeneutics, existentialism, phenomenology, and more – many biographers have attempted to narrate Derrida's life and aging according to his remarkable accomplishments. However, I maintain these are impossible to understand apart from the story of his Jewishness, and like Simmel in Berlin or Eiseley in Nebraska, this story is a narrative of spirit as much as mind.

Derrida the Jew

In retrospect, Derrida saw his life as a historical creation, one deeply linked to the complexities of Jewish identity, or as he says, "A series of contingencies have made of me a French Jew from Algeria born in the generation before the 'war of independence': so many singularities, even among Jews, and even among the Jews of Algeria. I was part of an extraordinary transformation of French Judaism in Algeria" (Derrida, 2007a, p. 35). The journey from his grandparents' generation in Algeria through to modern Parisian culture was borne by Derrida as a personal reckoning with the traces left by such contingencies in his name(s), body, speech, and sense of belonging. Speaking of the French language itself that deep well of his play and pleasure, Derrida says, "I have only one language, and, at the same time, in an at once singular and exemplary fashion, this language does not belong to me" (Derrida, 2007a, p. 39). In musing on her similar background as an Algerian Jew, French philosopher and feminist Hélène Cixous recalls:

> We were gripped by a circus feeling. We would see so many of those let's call them "Algerian Jews" - for the sake of brevity - performing their high-wire act in the void. Spangled in French but sporting kippas we called skullcaps, out they swung, having let go of the bar of their old culture, left it far behind them, in Morocco [sic], swimming across the abyss arms reach out for the other trapeze, the must-desired French, but there's France, hostile snatching it back. The Jewish trapezists cling to the void. A community out of step with the times. (Cixous, 2004, p. 115)

What began to mark Derrida's identity as a Jew, therefore, was this swinging within a void that was different from many of his contemporaries in France and their engagement with their Jewishness; for example, Claude Lévi-Strauss, Emmanuel Levinas, André Gluckmann, and Bernard-Henri Levy. One consistently senses in Derrida's work a gnawing uncertainty that ran throughout his struggle to reconcile how his Jewish background and identity were rooted to his philosophical world-view, and how, indeed, his embrace of deconstruction had an air of rabbinical delight in dancing around incomplete truths, preferring to leave their finalities up to God.

It is difficult not to sidestep the connective tissue between Derrida's scholarship and his soulful Jewishness, because of his constant denials of it, befuddling his critics and biographers alike who became ever more curious at rooting out Derrida, the Jew. Until the latter part of his career, Derrida responded to questions about the influence of his Jewish background with obscure gestures and disconnected clues. He had even suggested that his silence about being Jewish really was a mark of his being the "most Jewish" or, as Siegumfeldt comments, a way of "safeguarding the Jew in oneself" (Siegumfeldt, 2013, p. 395). As Siegumfeldt also points out, Derrida's childhood experiences made him wary of identifying with any community, including Jewish ones (Siegumfeldt, 2013, p. 393). In some instances, Derrida is quite explicit about this position: "Though I was born a Jew, I do not live or think within a living Jewish tradition. So that if there is a Judaic dimension to my thinking . . . this has never assumed the form of an explicit fidelity or debt to that culture" (Kearney, 1984, p. 107). Elsewhere, he admits that his guarded if not silent relationship with Judaism was a calculated distance, "I had to keep myself from Judaism in order to retain within myself something that I provisionally called 'jewishness'" (Derrida, 2007b, p. 7).

These and other statements about being Jewish without Judaism are discussed by Gideon Ofrat in his biography, *The Jewish Derrida* (Ofrat, 2001), leading critics such as Richard A. Cohen, in reviewing the book and the thesis that the absence of Judaism is constitutive of Derrida's Jewishness, to lambast both for presenting a stereotyping cliche of Jewishness itself (as never-settling wanderer, outsider, and other). For Cohen, Ofrat's book (and by implication other biographers) convinces him that "Derrida knows next to nothing, and wrote nothing serious or important, about the Judaism he never learned or practiced" (Cohen, 2003, p. 153). Cohen is not alone is accusing Derrida of a Jewish idealism, of fixing a radical alterity and critique of Enlightenment Reason to Judaism, without deeper historical context nor recourse to actual Jewish texts. As early as *Writing and Difference*, Derrida most famously asks: "Are we Jews? Are we Greeks? We live in the difference between the Jew and the Greek, which is perhaps the unity of what is called history" (Derrida, 1978, p. 153), as if Jerusalem and Athens launched the philosophical lineages whose grandness was created in their opposition to each other.[1]

By enjoying a position of self-proclaimed marginality between Jew and Greek, or outside of both Jerusalem and Athens, Derrida could engage with his Jewishness through playful textual strategies, metaphors, and imagery. Alan Megill makes this point when he says that "Derrida's appeal to Judaism as a marginal tradition, present within the interstices and along the edges of the "Western" tradition, gives his writings a much greater sense of alienation from that tradition than one finds in Nietzsche and Heidegger" (Megill, 1985, p. 303). Other critics have linked Derrida's work to Talmudic principles (Handelman, 1982) and the Kabbalah (Bannet, 1989; Wolfson, 2002). In *Glas* 1986, Derrida's critique of Hegel, the pages are divided like the Torah, such that, according to Shakespeare, "The Jewish scroll seems to be an image of a writing which will not allow itself to be mastered by the monologue of the philosophical system" (Shakespeare, 1998, p. 243). In 'A Silkworm of One's Own' (Derrida, 1996), Derrida evokes his father's silk *tallith* (Jewish prayer shawl) and the meaningfulness of its touch, memory, and timelessness. These examples align with what Emilie Kutash (2014) considers to be Derrida's *teshuvah*, a Hebrew term signifying a person's spiritual return to Judaism, which she sees as evident in his circular style with "synchronic structures" linked to each other, along with "sparks of judeity" that allow him to find his *hors-texte* (place outside of writing). She sees this happening in several ways. One is Derrida's use of multiple voices and "mouthpieces," which is a Talmudic tradition "where one reads on almost every page the opinion of one sage in the name of another." Another is "The agonizing and Talmudic '*mahloket*' that Derrida engages in with interlocutors, his internal debates and doubts, his never-ending and never dogmatic self-dialectic, has Talmudic precedent in method if it is not commensurate with other features of the oral tradition."

The Talmudic *mahloket* is a style of argument through productive conflict, by which rabbinical scholars create animated dialogue directed at spiritual discovery and theological understanding. Debates about whether or not Derrida was a Jewish philosopher or engaged in Jewish textual and argumentative styles are important, for leavening evidence of his actual fidelity to Judaism despite his denials. But as we have already seen, in Derrida's denials there lay a particularly troubled and profound relationship drawn between Judaism and his own Jewishness, embedded in his interlayered metaphysical geography of outside, alternative, and silenced places. In the next section, we explore these more fully in relation to Derrida's deconstructive methodology, for which he is best known.

The Jewishness of deconstruction

Deconstruction, while not a philosophy, as Derrida insisted, is an approach to philosophy, a radical unveiling of the biases, binaries, and hierarchies that transform thought into truth. It shares with the work of Nietzsche, Foucault, and Deleuze a counter-strategy that skirts debating with various philosophies in favor of locating them within certain historical Eurocentric traditions, whose meanings and modes of significance exceed their texts. However, the work of deconstruction is not simply to overturn, since this might "leave the previous field untouched, leaving one no hold on the previous opposition, thereby preventing any means of *intervening* in the field effectively" (Derrida, 1981, p. 41). Rather, the deconstructionist also pursues "the irruptive emergence of a new 'concept,' a concept that can no longer be, and never could be, included in the previous regime" (Ibid., p. 41). In Derrida's writing, deconstruction transforms the core essentials sedimented in philosophical discourse into a language of dissonance, violence, indeterminacy, pluralism, and suspicion. However, the new concept that is expected to emerge from the exercise of deconstruction is more elusive in Derrida's work, because it bears the burden of representing the unrepresentable "other" that lies beyond language itself. The concept is a product of relentless argument and ineffable mystery at the same time.

Who, then, is the deconstructionist, if they are a philosopher without a philosophy, or an interpreter outside of interpretation? And where, if anywhere, is the deconstructed space of thought and spirit from which one can contemplate truth and justice without the interference of Eurocentric orders of signification? In his early work, *Writing and Difference*, Derrida looks to the different interpretive figures of the poet and the rabbi, neither of whom, as Shakespeare says, "can claim mastery of meaning; both are faced with a radical illegibility at the heart of being" (Shakespeare, 1998, p. 245). Yet, Derrida's tear through the archive of European philosophy left critics wondering with what he intended to replace it. As Kutash (2014) notes, "By the nineties, his [Derrida's] own ongoing 'parricide' of the patrimony of Western metaphysics had done its lethal work." The most obvious and creative response was to look again at Derrida's Jewishness to see where, if or how it might correspond to the project of deconstruction. Siegumfeldt sums up this movement by noting about Derrida that "While his Jewishness belongs to the most obscure and illegible part of his private life, substantial aspects of his work articulate the affiliation and translate it into universal structures that have visibly marked deconstructive theory" (Siegumfeldt, 2013, p. 392). And, as suggested above, Jewish themes and images run throughout Derrida's work, but within the contrary work of deconstruction, he seems to set the logics and binaries of European philosophy against Jewish themes of exile, silencing, testimony, and wonder. Shakespeare says that such themes signify that, "for Derrida Judaism witnesses to a divine order which suspends the violence inherent in myths of purity, and to a justice which transcends the order of right" (Shakespeare, 1998, p. 248). Derrida also borrowed from his Jewish contemporary philosopher, Emmanuel Levinas, an ethical perspective on deconstruction that involved concepts of forgiveness, hope, and morality (see Critchley, 2014; Srajek, 1998). Kutash (2014) adds that Levinas, and his Jewish "ethics beyond ethics" brought "a moral urgency onto the playing field, and this accrues an increasingly compelling intensity for Derrida," who later, "freely adopts Levinas to jump-start his own ethical 'otherness,' outside of philosophical/public discourse."

A good example of the correspondence between Jewish traditions, ethics, and the objectives of deconstruction can be found in Derrida's book *Gift of Death* (Derrida, 1995), where he elaborates the meaning of Abraham's willingness to sacrifice his son Isaac for God with reference to the question of faith espoused by Søren Kierkegaard (*Fear and Trembling*, 1941). Here, Derrida seems to find at the scene of biblical Mount Moriah the possibility of an outside, deconstructed space in the Abrahamic drama, that bespeaks to him a purity untouched by language or ambivalence. God commands Abraham who in turn responds without question or hesitation that he is fully present and prepared to carry out God's test of faith, even if the request made of Abraham is so unlawful and cruel, and ultimately, reversed. But Derrida admires these silent perils of devotion and responsibility and relates them to his own work: "By preferring my work, simply by giving it my time and attention, by preferring my activity as a citizen or as a professorial and professional philosopher, writing, and speaking here in a public language, French in my case, I am perhaps fulfilling my duty. But I am sacrificing and betraying at every moment all my other obligations" (Derrida, 1995, p. 69). As Kutash comments, "The moment of avowal at Moriah, then, holds significance for Derrida as a template for the possibility of a secret self that is genuinely and truly 'outside'" (Kutash, 2019, p. 5).[2]

If, in Judaism, Derrida sought the metaphysical terrain of deconstruction that included his own ambivalent, hide-and-seek relationship with his Jewishness, what did this mean for his own soulful aging? Where did the driving obsession with a marginal, outside space of thought, negotiated between the Greek/Western philosophical lineages and the timeless Judaic sacred texts and traditions, leave *him*? In his own words, Derrida said he often felt like a *Marrano* (Cixous, 2004; Kutash, 2019) (a term for late-medieval Jews in the Iberian Peninsula who had to convert to Christianity and were often expelled from their communities, but still secretly practiced Jewish customs and beliefs). The *Marrano* does indeed characterize the ultimately liminal figure, caught between cultures, places, faiths, and identities, a lonely exteriority, and coerced impoverishment of belonging. This sentiment, also found in *Monolingualism of the Other* (Derrida, 1998) and *Circumfession* (Derrida, 1993), portends a certain humility and isolation. Again Kutash (2014) comments about Derrida:

> Overexposed to Western literature and underexposed to the oral and written traditions and practices of his own people, Derrida has picked his way out of the debris of Western culture. At the end of his life, he has exhausted what he calls his 'Peloponnesian' weavings. Having removed all of the idols of Western philosophical discourse in the last of his writings and lectures, bereft of conceptual balm, his Judaism has gathered momentum and, in proportion to it, he trembles.

In many ways, then, Derrida's personal and intellectual struggles created his own desert, a space alone and secretive, somewhat lost and uncertain, speaking a language that was not his own and, in Caputo's terms, participating in 'religion without religion' (Caputo, 1997). Thus, Cixous asks,

> So where to find oneself? Will he ever find himself? Where? Save in prison. In prison? What next? Another illusion? It is this solitude that dogs him, so trusty, so far away so close.
>
> In prison outside
>
> Alone with himself. (2004, pp. 119, 121)

But the ordeal of wandering in the desert for Jews is rewarded with settling in a God-given homeland, a place of prayer and belonging whereby the lonely desert takes up residence inside the soul of every Jew. This is a theme to be explored in the following concluding section.

Derrida as Abraham

On the one hand, few modern, including Jewish, philosophers have been so questioned about the influences of their religious and spiritual backgrounds as has Jacques Derrida.[3] The debates around his appropriations of rabbinical, Talmudic, and Kabbalistic principles continue far beyond his death in 2004 (e.g., Baring & Gordon, 2014) as do interrogations about what Derrida meant by "Jewishness" (he spelled it with small 'j') and the language he used to frame his relationship to it (Gaon, 2014). On the other hand, Derrida's adroit shuffling around the subject suggests not only his own ambivalence, while attempting to express some kind of coherent and less defensive narrative about being and writing as a Jew, but also a soulful coming-to-terms with it as a gift of his aging, not just his scholarship. In my view, he should be viewed as gerontologically important for this reason.

There are two texts (the second in the next section) that, in particular, illustrate how Derrida the elder made of his Jewishness an internal, spiritual reckoning. The first is *Judeities: Questions for Jacques Derrida*, (Bergo, Cohen & Zagury-Orly, Derrida, 2007b), a publication of proceedings from a conference at the Jewish Community Center in Paris in 2000 (the English version only contains some of the original French essays). Derrida's opening paper, "Abraham, the Other," is, among other things, a moving confession of his life as a Jew and how, at that point, he and his Jewishness had grown closer together and find affinity in his work. As he introduces the paper, "Early on, and for a long time I have trembled, I still tremble, before the title of this conference (questions addressed to me! and concerning *judeities*!) and never has the privilege of a conference apparently addressed to me intimidated, worried, or flustered me this much, to the point of leaving me with the feeling that a grave misunderstanding threatened to make me forget how much I feel, and will always feel, out of place in speaking of it" (p. 4). This is an especially reflective moment about the "it" (his Jewishness) since Derrida admits, "I had to keep myself from Judaism in order to retain within myself something that I provisionally called jewishness" (p. 6). He further claims that two "appellations" have driven his life: "These are, so far as I know, the only two words about which I have relentlessly sought to find out, in the darkness of my memory, where, when, and how their epiphany came to light for me, gave birth for me – as far as I am concerned" (p. 8), they are "*God-- and Jew*" (p. 8). While he remains mysterious about such an epiphany and the fuller explanation of these two appellations, his statement about them is still powerful, although we know that the second appellation, Jew, was already socially and politically defined for Derrida since childhood as laden with negative meaning.

In the remainder of the paper, Derrida moves artfully around his Jewishness, expanding and contracting it, while folding it into shapes and patterns that bespeak a genuine search for faith, outside the guise of Western reason. For Derrida, who feels both "less jewish *and* more jewish than the Jew, as scarcely Jewish and as superlatively Jewish as possible," this "overbidding of an excess never stops": "I have found it everywhere; it has found me everywhere, and one could locate a thousand signs in writings and teachings, in arguments that I did not direct – neither in appearance, nor in reality – toward the theme of any jewish question" (p. 16). Derrida prefers to be "more jewish" if it means being more universally representative of humankind, but this means being "less jewish" in terms of belonging to the set roles and definitions of a Jewish community, or nation. This is also why he denounces Sartre's distinction between authentic and inauthentic Jews (p. 24). Rather, Derrida wishes to call himself a Jew without being concerned if he is an authentic, inauthentic, quasi, (or any other) kind of Jew (p. 30), leaning again to the model of Abraham, in saying, "here I am," without question, without knowing what will be asked of him.

> And what sense can there be in saying, in affirming, in signing, and maintaining a "here I am," me as a Jew, beyond sense and meaning? In saying "here I am," and insisting, that I know that perhaps I have not been called, and that perhaps I will never know it is not me who has been called. Not yet. Perhaps in a future to come, but not yet. (pp. 30–31)

Commenting on Derrida's deeply personal lecture and book chapter, Siegumfeldt summarizes by saying, "for the first time he [Derrida] ascribes the aporetic structure of his thinking to a particular propensity for indeterminacy, which he aligns not with Judaism in any of its doctrinal forms but with his own, somewhat idiosyncratic, experience of being Jewish" (Siegumfeldt, 2013, p. 385). Further, "He himself had been circling around the notion of Jewishness for so long, repeatedly approaching it, but always with reserve, always, at least in public, from the safe distance afforded by a deconstructive stance. The time had now come to lay his cards on the table" (p. 391). And compared to the scattered passages in Derrida's earlier *Circumfession*, "Abraham, the other" is a soul-bearing clarification of Derrida's career *as* a Jew (not a Marrano), from his perspective as a 70-year-old veteran of the major philosophical debates of his time. Indeed, Siegumfeldt asks if the confessions of the Paris 2000 conference now "mean that we can classify deconstruction as, simply, 'Jewish'" (Siegumfeldt, 2013, p. 387).

Jewish survival and saying yes to life

Derrida's essay "Abraham, the other," marks being Jewish for him as a source of both intellectual and spiritual empowerment, because, for him, the "oscillation" and "undecidability" that characterizes it, as he says, "has conditioned the decisions and the responsibilities that have imprinted themselves upon my life. Moreover, it structures the most formalized, the most resistant, the most irreducible logic of all the discourses I believed I had to endorse endorse" (Derrida, 2007b, p. 33). There is also, within this Jewishness, a messianic promise of emancipation and hope for the future, the "to-come" which "will decide what 'jew', 'judaism', or 'jewishness' will have signified" for him (p. 33). This optimism connects Derrida's "Abraham, the other" to the second text I wish to discuss to conclude this essay, which is the book *Learning to Live Finally: The Last Interview* (Derrida, 2007a) (originally published in *Le Monde* and titled "I am a War with Myself"), based on Derrida's interview (with Jean Birnbaum) a few weeks before he died on October 9, 2004.

By the time of this interview, Derrida was aware that he had a terminal illness (pancreatic cancer) and likely facing his end, and so his remarks on death, survivorship, and legacy are poignant and revelatory. There is also a sense of a certain contentment, finally, with being a Jewish philosopher (outside of philosophy). Birnbaum says that Derrida is "a thinker whose entire work pays homage to the subversive intensity of existence" (Derrida, 2007a, p. 9). But this "subversive intensity," that had inspired Derrida's fervent expeditions to the margins of civilized thought and beyond, also became a soulful journey of self-realization for his spiritual identity as a Jew. When Derrida talks about his survival, or what might survive when he's gone, one can hear aging Jewish wisdom at its core, for to survive as a Jew or to have one's work as a Jew survive, means the survival of Judaism itself, against a world driven to eradicate it. He says "I have always been interested in this theme of survival, the meaning of which is not to be added on to living and dying. It is originary: life is living on, life is survival" (p. 26).[4] Not only does he hope his work will keep the "debate alive" among the thinkers of his generation and for the future, but he sees in his writing the possibility of a timeless legacy: "I leave a piece of paper behind, I go away, I die: it is impossible to escape this structure, it is the unchanging form of my life . . .. I live my death in writing" (p. 33).

Further, and what I find to be the most spiritually Jewish statements of all, just as survival for Derrida is about living and the future, so "deconstruction is always on the side of the *yes*, on the side of the affirmation of life" (p. 51, original emphasis). Despite Derrida's writings on mourning and death in his later years, and all the critics' claims against him for being nihilistic and intellectually destructive,[5] here the aged philosopher is offering an Abrahamic assessment of his work, one of offering himself without reservation to the greater forces of 'life.' As Derrida says,

> My discourse is not a discourse of death, but, on the contrary, the affirmation of a living being who prefers living and thus surviving to death, because survival is not simply that which remains but the most intense life possible. I am never more haunted by the necessity of dying than in moments of happiness and joy. To feel joy and weep over the death that awaits me are for me the same thing. When I recall my life, I tend to think that I have had the good fortune to love even the unhappy moments of my life, and to bless them. (p. 52)

These comments about life and death, love and survival, are not simply a parallel to Frankl's (1946, 2021) remarkable optimism about the survival of the Jewish spirit, but an expression of deeper roots in Jewish teaching about fearless trust and Godly faith. While "saying yes to life" has also taken on a distorted meaning in some quarters of Jewish thought as distinguishing Jews from their enemies, cast as cults of death, it is steeped in a more spiritual belief that life is a gift, a *mitzvah*, with which Jews are blessed to commit acts of *Tikun Olam* (to "repair the world"), to care for the world through justice and compassion. And for all his meticulous dismantling the philosophies, arts, and literatures that framed the century in which he lived and the culture he both loved and defied, perhaps, in the end, assembling them together for a higher and future purpose might have been Derrida's soulful mission after all.

Derrida decided to write his own brief funeral address, to be read by his son Pierre, 3 days after his death (October 9, 2004).

> He asks me to thank you for coming and to bless you, he begs you not to be mournful, to think only if the many happy moments which you gave him the chance of sharing with you. Smile at me, he says, as I will have smiled at you till the end. Always prefer life and never cease affirming survival.

L'chaim! (to life) Jacques Élie Derrida.

Notes

1. Philosopher Jean-Luc Nancy, one of Derrida's students, argued that the project of deconstruction is less of one between Jewish and Greek philosophies, than about the critique of Christianity (2008). However, the image of this philosophical opposition assumes that Jewish scholars played no role in the development of modern European thought and in the project of the Enlightenment itself. To the contrary Spinoza (Baruch de Spinoza), the sixteenth-century Jewish, Dutch philosopher, created a rationalistic pantheistic vision of the universe. Another often-cited example is Moses Mendelssohn's book *Jerusalem* originally published in 1783 (Mendelssohn, 1983), that argues for the compatibility between the tolerance of Judaism and the philosophical and political ideals of (Enlightenment) Reason (see Feiner, 2004).
2. Anidjar (2002) also points out that the importance of "the Abrahamic" to Derrida's ideas on religion and the politics of difference is that it brings into focus three major monotheistic world religions (Judaism, Christianity, Islam) and is thus "welcoming" and "hospitable" as a foundation for inter-faith dialogue and intersecting identities (for Derrida, Arab-Jew). Of course today the biblical site of Mount Moriah (and the Temple Mount atop of it) in Jerusalem remains one of the most troubled places of heated contestation.
3. This culture of interrogation includes, in part, the controversies around Derrida's engagement with Martin Heidegger's sympathies with Nazism (Derrida, 1989), and his friend philosopher Paul de Man and the discovery of his collaborative and anti-Semitic journalism in Nazi occupied Belgium (Derrida, 1990; Weiner, 1989). See also Derrida's interview with Michal Ben-Naftali in Jerusalem (1998).
4. Neither Derrida's wife, Marguerite Aucouturier (who died in 2020 from COVID-19 infection) nor his sons by her, by Jewish tradition, are Jewish, hence his Jewish lineage was not to be carried forth.
5. Some of these criticisms were repeated in various obituaries and tributes to Derrida in the media after he died, the worst of which was *The Times (of London)* jokingly suggesting that, since Derrida and his followers doubted the realities of existence, perhaps he had not really died (*The Times,* October 11, 2004).

Disclosure statement

No potential conflict of interest was reported by the author.

ORCID

Stephen Katz http://orcid.org/0000-0001-7403-6696

References

Anidjar, G. (Ed.). (2002). *Acts of Religion, Jacques Derrida*. Routledge.

Bannet, E. T. (1989). *Structuralism and the logic of dissent*. Macmillan.

Baring, E., & Gordon, P. E. (2014). *The Trace of God: Derrida and Religion*. Indiana University Press.

Ben-Naftali, M. (1998). An interview with Jacques Derrida. M. Ron (Ed.) *Yad Vashem (Jerusalem)*. Jan 8/1998. 1–29

Caputo, J. D. (1997). The prayers and tears of Jacques Derrida. religion without religion. *Theology Today-Pennsylvania*, *56*, 146–147

Cixous, H. (2004). *Portrait of Jacques Derrida as a young Jewish Saint*. (B. B. Brahic, Ed.). Columbia University Press.

Cohen, R. A. (2003). Review*the Jewish Derrida* (Gideon Ofrat, 2001). *Shofar: An Interdisciplinary Journal of Jewish Studies*, *21*(2), 153–155. https://doi.org/10.1353/sho.2002.0138

Critchley, S. (2014). *The ethics of deconstruction: Derrida and Levinas*. Edinburgh University Press.

Derrida, J. (1978). *Writing and Difference*. (A. Bass, Ed.). University of Chicago Press.

Derrida, J. (1981). *Positions*. (A. Bass, Ed.). The University of Chicago Press.

Derrida, J. (1986). *Glas*. (J. P. Leavey Jr. and R. Rand, Eds.). University of Nebraska Press.

Derrida, J. (1989). *Of spirit: Heidegger & the question*. (G. Bennington & R. Bowlby, Eds.). University Press.

Derrida, J. (1990). *Memoires for Paul de Man*. (C. Lindsay, J. Culler, E. Cadava, & P. Kamuf, Eds.). Columbia University Press.

Derrida, J. (1993). Circumfession. In G. Bennington (Ed.), *Jacques Derrida* (pp. 3–315). The University of Chicago Press.

Derrida, J. (1995). *The gift of death*. (D. Wills, Ed.). University of Chicago Press.

Derrida, J. 1996. A Silkworm of one's own (points of view stitched on the other veil). Ed. G. Bennington. *Oxford Literary Review*, *18*(½), 3–65.https://doi.org/10.3366/olr.1996.002

Derrida, J. (1998). *Monolingualism of the Other: Or, the Prosthesis of Origin*. (P. Mensah, Ed.). Stanford University Press.

Derrida, J. (2007a). *Learning to live finally: The last interview*. (P.-A. Brault & M. Naas, Eds.). Palgrave Macmillan.

Derrida, J. (2007b). Abraham, the other. In B. Bergo, J. Cohen, & R. Zagury-Orly (Eds.), *Judeities: Questions for Jacques Derrida* (pp. 1–35). Fordham University Press.

Derrida (documentary film), 2002, directors Kirby Dick and Amy Ziering, Zeitgeist Films.

Eiseley, L. (1957). *The Immense Journey*. Random House.

Feiner, S. (2004). *The jewish enlightenment*. (C. Naor, Ed.). University of Pennsylvania Press.

Frankl, V. E. (1946). *Yes to life: In spite of everything*. Beacon Press.

Frisby, D. (1992). *Simmel and since: Essays on Georg Simmel's social theory*. Routledge.

Gaon, S. (2014). 'As if' there were a 'Jew': The (non)existence of deconstructive Responsibility. *Derrida Today*, *7*(1), 44–58. https://doi.org/10.3366/drt.2014.0076

Geertz, C. (1988). *Works and Lives: The anthropologist as author*. Polity Press.

Gornick, V. (2008). *The men in my life*. MIT Press (A Boston Review Book).

Handelman, S. (1982). *The slayers of Moses*. State University of New York Press.

Kearney, R. (1984). *Dialogues with contemporary thinkers*. Manchester University Press.

Kierkegaard, S. (1941). *Fear and Trembling*, trans. W. Lowrie. Princeton University Press.

Kutash, E. (2014). The *Teshuvah* of Jacques Derrida: Judaism *Hors-texte*. *Journal of Textual Reasoning*, *8*(1), online. https://jtr.shanti.virginia.edu/volume-8-number-1/the-teshuvah-of-jacques-derrida-judaism-hors-texte/

Kutash, E. Jacques Derrida: The double liminality of a philosophical Marrano. (2019). *Religions, 10*(2), 1–12. (SP)68. https://doi.org/10.3390/rel10020068

Megill, A. (1985). *Prophets of extremity: Nietzsche, Heidegger, Foucault, Derrida.* University of California Press.

Mendelssohn, M. (1983). *Jerusalem: Or on Religion Power and Judaism.* (A. Arkush Trans.). Brandeis University Press.

Nancy, J. -L. (2008). *Dis-enclosure: The deconstruction of Christianity.* (B. Bergo, G. Malenfant, & M. B. Smith, Eds.). Fordham University Press.

Ofrat, G. (2001). *The Jewish Derrida.* (P. Kidron, Ed.). Syracuse University Press.

Peeters, B. (2012). *Derrida: A biography.* Polity Press.

Rabinow, P. (1996). *Making PCR: A story of biotechnology.* University of Chicago Press.

Salmon, P. (2020). *An event, Perhaps: A biography of Jacques Derrida.* Verso Books.

Shakespeare, S. (1998). Thinking about "Fire": Derrida and Judaism. *Literature and Theology, 12*(3), 242–255. https://doi.org/10.1093/litthe/12.3.242

Siegumfeldt, I. -B. (2013). Difficult bond: Derrida and Jewishness. *Jewish Quarterly Review, 103* (5), 385–400. https://doi.org/10.1353/jqr.2013.0024

Simmel, G. (1971). The metropolis and mental life. In D. Levine Ed., *Georg Simmel: On individuality and social forms.* 1903 (pp. 324–339). Chicago University Press.

Srajek, M. C. (1998). *In the margins of deconstruction: Jewish Conceptions of ethics in Emmanuel Levinas and Jacques Derrida.* Springer Science+Business Media.

The Times (of London), Is Derrida Dead? A conceptual foundation for the deconstruction of mortality. Oct 11, 2004.

Weiner, J. (1989). The responsibilities of friendship: Jacques Derrida on Paul de man's collaboration. *Critical Inquiry, 15*(4), 797–803. https://doi.org/10.1086/448520

Wirth, L. (1938). Urbanism as a way of life. *The American Journal of Sociology, 44*(1), 1–24. https://doi.org/10.1086/217913

Wolfson, E. R. (2002). Assaulting the border: kabbalistic traces in the margins of Derrida. *Journal of the American Academy of Religion, 70*(3), 475–514. https://doi.org/10.1093/jaar/70.3.475

Soulful ageing - a lifetime cancer journey

Janice Ryan

ABSTRACT
Soulful Ageing - a lifetime cancer journey describes experiences of cancer and how such deely personal event in a lifetime provide a unique lens for understanding soulful ageing. The author shapes a descriptive journey with cancer at seventen and then again at sixrty years, and its spriitual awakenings, The health challenge of cancer over a lifetime strengthened faith, deepened a spiriutality, built on resileincy and fostered a heart of gratefulness.

I found myself diagnosed with cancer for the third time in my life; Hodgkins in 1979, Thyroid Cancer in 1988 and now Breast Cancer 2021. I know how fortunate I am to have gotten through the other cancers, but did I have the resiliency within me to face a third cancer and its unknowns. How was this experience going to be faced; within myself, with my adult son and daughter, siblings and friends Was there a way forward beyond fears and uncertainties to put all in perspective and live my best life? Of course, I was caught by anxiety and negative thoughts, but I had to teach myself again how to find peace beyond these intense emotions. I am a hopeful person and stubborn so I could use this determined personality to let cancer not take over my being. I wanted to manifest a positive outlook, yet again. I had to push myself through this difficult time and to survive the mental, emotional, and physical challenges that were to come. Soulful aging is a worthwhile spirit process I have embraced repeatedly as it has been so very nurturing during these very difficult times in my life. It allows you to reflect on your journey through a larger lens and encourages optimism, heart, positivity and draws on the strength of community and the love of the divine.

Soulful aging can uncover a pathway to meaning and understanding of life in its ultimate brevity. We eventually move away from a path that separates and divides into one liberating us from old garments of security, division and human pride. Instead, we embrace the frailty and unpredictability of the human condition, knowing that our own failures constantly disarm our righteousness.

How does Cancer and its medical journey throughout life shape a person's soul deeply and irredeemably? The positive legacy of journeying through cancer for me is a form of soulful aging. Soulful aging is recognizing community in the care and the healing of the body. The soul rises in wellness through community, compassion, and connections with strangers and friends. Cancer is all about love and soul.

My roots are in a large Irish Catholic family. We lived in our great grandparents' home, in uptown Saint John, New Brunswick. Me and my six siblings are the fifth generation in Canada after a wave of Irish immigration dating from the 1840's. Family, tradition and faith were essential cornerstones of lived experience. We were aware that each room held stories and memories of family. My great-grandfather had been a lawyer in Saint John, NB. His father before him had on arrival in Canada been a liquor merchant. The family had come from an Island off of the south of Ireland.The nuns had schooled my maternal great grandmother. Her mother died soon after she was born. Her father too was a liquor merchant who remarried and had three sons. Loss, death, illness, displacement, change and fortitude are parts of our family stories for generations. On my father's side of the Miramichi there were loggers and railway employees. My grandfather, on my paternal side, had a stint as mayor of Newcastle. His grandfather before him had been a tavern operator; killed in a political election fight in the community. For me these family stories gave breadth and depth to our history.

A professor once challenged me to see that we are not what we have done or who we are. We are the collective of who and what formed us. And so recounting stories of family characters and personal history reminds me of the threads weaved into each life from our own communities and inheritance. Soulful aging examines patterns: the legacy of all personal and familial struggles and disappointments, and the hope of births and beginnings which is part and parcel of the human journey.

I discovered an internal sense of joy when I was about five playing with a toy log cabin set. That moment of discovery, contentment and joy shaped an experience which I will name an eternal moment. The revelation of abandonment at five years was experienced in the threshold of my parents' bedroom where the sun streamed in and I felt at oneness, at home. I had received this new birthday gift and the sense of a world that could be built with sticks and surrounded with play farm animals was so full of satisfaction and pleasure as the sun gave the warmth and deep comfort of "just being there".

Another memorable childhood experience of the soul was in the exhilaration of flying high on a playground swing as the sun shone down and danced about on the tidal waters. I was transposed by a knowingness and resonance with exuberance and joy. The movement of the swing produced both a rush and a sense of freedom. The sound of the surf, the warm summer air with its saltiness and the soft sand took me out of myself into this moment. I remember how I did not want this feeling to end.

As a child I had occasions to be with my grandmother. When she would prepare a grilled cheese sandwich with mayonnaise for me; I felt nurtured, loved, cared for, and indulged. I remember hearing about God's great love as a child and that rivers, oceans, mountains and flowers and even bugs connote the abundance of the divine in our world. The sense of receiving abundant love and nurturing was certainly felt downstairs in that precious time with my grandmother.

On another occasion when I was sick, my grandmother took me to a local west side beach to enjoy an ice cream. I thought of this moment and embraced this memory before the delivery of each of my children. As the due date was coming ever so near, I went to the local ice cream shop savoring the soft serve as I paused, readied, and prepared myself to go forth and give birth. Life just has these moments of largeness where we get to dwell in time and relish it.

My sense of the spiritual began in the chaos and activity of such a busy home with seven siblings, parents, and grandmother. In order to keep out of trouble, I kept quiet. Being quiet or separate was for me a practiced way of avoiding a fight or squabble. I developed this interior self perhaps out of personality, observation and an intuitive side. As a child, I was drawn to my "own" even as we were of one household. I treasured my own thoughts and emotions, the quiet and magic of moments at the lake or at the seashore, the abundance and care we enjoyed in family and church in sacred and holiday celebrations, the peace of practicing piano and enjoying music, the ecstatic feeling of running the fields at our country place or climbing a tree and peering down. I savored running on hot sand at a seaside beach or at our camp at Loch Lomand Lake. I always had my sisters as friends and knowing they were there was implicitly part of my fullest sense of being in the world. This sense of being cocooned in this tight family still remains even after our parents have gone. Within these familial relationships there remains a family sensibility: acceptance and challenge, differences and similarities, responsibility and care, and a common capacity to encircle one another in crisis, illness, or challenge.

We begin in youth and adulthood with frameworks for life and learning. Soulful aging lets go of definitions that are rigid and confining and embraces wider and broader approaches, beliefs, and perspectives. It is an unencumbered inner listening of self and other and a re-listening again and again for inner truths. It is both a process and a state of giving over all knowing to the transcendent and a recognition of our utter vulnerability and place in the flow. There is both an embrace of the wildness of creation in all its particularity and our inter-being with all.

For me intuition, curiosity, and an interest in stories were a natural way to be and to learn. I would admire the historical prints on the wall as a child and marvel and look for detail in, Daniel and the Lion's Den or a scenic black and white pastoral scene of herds from the Hebrides. We were surrounded by the fine furniture my great grandfather had acquired; a china cabinet, buffet or twelve-person oak table where we dined at Christmas and Easter dinners. Though my parents were of middle income the house portrayed that history of comfort and wealth. The historic house was a two-story wooden structure that housed the stories and lives of generations. As a teenager I would peruse the older things and examine the silver hairbrush and comb, receipts and correspondence, old books, and old photos for clues to the life before us. In the downstairs living room, there was a piano against the wall where we practiced daily amid a classic room of rugs, tapestry, and a large golden mirror over a marble fireplace. Each corner had memories and mysteries of lives spent and configured in this living space.

My own parents were not attached to history and lived in the present. Life in a big family was evolving and constant with personal decisions and challenges. As children, we would huddle in the vestibule of our home after returning from a day at school and smell the baking wafting through the air. We would run up the sixteen stairs to the second floor where we primarily resided, anxious to swap our school clothes for play duds, grabbing an apple, checking to see if there was a cookie or square ready and then running out to play "around the block" Our grandmother lived with us and was a significant part of our lives and daily interactions. She might call us into her bedroom and ask us to thread a needle or invite us to sample a homemade donut. My mother, who ran the household exuded a traditional, busy, focused, capable manner as she managed all the family daily affairs and put our meals on the table.

As a child I was cocooned in this large family. I had five sisters and a younger brother. My mother was a nurse and my father a police officer. Order and routines were present, and the notion of individual will and decisions negligible until our university days. We grew up with our siblings as friends and in a tight knit community. My mother and father did not signal to any of us a particular advantage but together their parental style was of pairing siblings as partners, using discipline and correction, teaching, or guiding over family conversations and we knew their expectations. As a child and pre-teen, I felt safe; as all the basic needs were met, fun was had, and routine and play were the norm.

At age seventeen I was diagnosed with Hodgkin's Disease. The fear created by this cancer gripped my being. I did feel alone, I did fear death. Thankfully, I had a family who supported me, and I had a developing sense of faith which gave me strength. Today, all these years later, I remember parts of that cancer experience vividly. Memory is a powerful way of linking thoughts, emotions and of creating meaning and understanding of the myriad of life events and the diverse learnings and challenges. For some, memory can quicken fear and pessimism. For me, memory gives comfort and even hope.

I remember looking into the mirror of an antique bureau in our shared bedroom with my twin sisters. I was alone and noticed a lump on my collarbone. I showed it to my mother and after examining it, she said plainly, without alarm, we would see a doctor about it. I did see the family physician and eventually a specialist. A battery of tests and surgical interventions ensued before I understood that the word "cancer" was even being discussed. Only later in the journey did I learn the severity of my illness.

I was seventeen years old at diagnosis and several months later I would celebrate my birthday. I can recall the female oncologist telling me the diagnosis and its name. I remember how clear and direct her manner was and how that helped me have confidence in the future and in hope. Hope is another word that is laden with so much meaning. Hope is something we can hold onto amid incredible change, uncertainty, and unknowns.

After my Hodgkins diagnosis in 1979, I began chemotherapy. I remember chemo sessions were taken at the General Hospital in the oncology ward. In my young mind, this was a place of death and I felt I did not belong there. I did not want to see the sick and did not want to think of myself as them. And the treatments were hard on the body. I was so sick after each session with its effect lasting for days. I remember my mother being there, and her support and help, wetting a cloth for my head and face. I also remember the nurses being there after each session, offering a friendly, kind manner which supported me too.

My experience was shaped by the strength of my mother's heart and her certainty and compassion when she affirmed at the outset "you will be ok" and "you will not lose your hair" as I cried in fear and trepidation. I think she resolutely faced this threat as much as I. Or perhaps her experience was just as profound. She perhaps worried more and feared more for me. I would have moments where I would doubt but then return to her positive clear message and the command and certainty the oncologist evoked.

I have the memory of standing over a basin being sick. And of the dry heaves, the sound of it after my stomach emptied. And the convulsions continued and the overnight observation in hospital ensued. But I so wanted to be at home and not in the hospital. I so wanted to be picked up at daybreak for discharge. The child-adult wanted the flight out of the hospital with such an urgency. So much emotional energy was expended by my parents dealing with this crisis. And so many years later, I came to know how much both my parents and family went through in supporting me, in hiding things from me, in facing cancer and what it meant for them. They struggled to meet my needs but at the same time had the rest of the family to tend to. They had pressing financial and work obligations. This cancer affected the whole family. At seventeen, I perhaps didn't fully comprehend this but as the years passed I gained a deep appreciation for how cancer affected them as well.

Soulful aging permits joy to reign without condemnation of self or other. Soulful aging embraces a wide spectrum of life; from plant to animal to human life, all connected to this one inexplicable cosmos of life. Cancer points to death and life at the same time; it is holding contradictions as one whole beingness that we again learn and relearn to be and to live.

Truly I was one of seven; indistinguishable even to myself as a person or personality. My mother and father had a parenting style that focused on building family time and friendships and belonging amongst us. We all took piano lessons, speed skated, swam with our father, played hockey on the pond, and practiced tennis together on many courts. These collective activities changed and flowed from one season to another. Experiences of family were safe, secure, routine, and enjoyed as one of many. I would be rarely but sometimes distinguished from the many in school, music or in sport. I was deemed the quiet one, the shy one, having musicality, and attempted to please parental expectations with good marks, a competitive spirit and engaging fully in school activities including student council, choirs, musicals, band, field hockey, badminton, field hockey, tennis etc.

One of these reflective moments brought a closer sense of God into my life. As a Catholic family we went to weekly Mass. Once in a while, we would be asked to kneel and our father would lead us in rosary and on Saturdays we were taken to confession lining up one behind each other, reluctantly. Yet God was curiously found not in church nor rosary but in my bedroom shared with siblings. I experienced the dark night of being with cancer without any consolation or not knowing how to ask for that. I cried and felt deeply alone in my bed. In that moment, I experienced what would be described as a loving presence coming near and of deep consolation. I had not understood how a spiritual presence was felt but experienced an inner recognition of extraordinary love. This presence which I deemed as the God of our faith was felt as deep peace and deep presence and gave calm and reassurance.

There were times where my mother's presence was stalwart and I knew her power and her strength, which aided my inner strength. We never talked about my experience of cancer. I felt her presence was akin to God's presence at this time; silent, powerful, knowing, and with a command unspoken word to "just do it". I think of myself as a child as quiet, shy, disengaged, and emotional. I did not lose these qualities but rather added to them a capacity to endure, to overcome, to rise above, to seek the good, to pursue the happy, to give gratitude, to thank God for small things, to celebrate being alive in the moment.

My birthday and chemotherapy treatment was planned on that day, December 27. My blood was too low for treatment, and I was so thankful, but I remember the eyes and compassion of the oncologist as he saw my tears well up. There were many experiences where I felt "emotion" and saw "the compassion of others" which helped me to carry feelings unstated. I would hear whisperings and discussions between my mother and grandmother about me. These hushed communications engendered the deep sense of matriarchal care but also reinforced the isolation I felt in this cancer story. I received loads of prayer cards from neighbors and strangers. I knew that I was in a life and death encounter. And yet rebuffed directions from medical personnel in small ways where I could. I would wash my hair rebelliously when I was told not to. I could get away with a parental spoil that normally would be a No. My father bought a tiny Christmas tree for me (my own) which was a powerful sign of hope. It was not often that we had our "own" but here was this small, beautiful tree I could decorate. We as siblings shared clothes, food, activities, friends yet I carried on not talking nor sharing any stories of my experience. Only once did I write to my sister about my treatment as she was at university. And yet my mother devoted so much time with me alone at the hospital or my favorite uncle came to visit me. Small acts of graciousness resonated deeply at this time. I felt valued and worthy of value.

The spiritual in soulful aging knows ineffable love. It embraces the always intangible divine moment of deep connection and humanity. Both the divine and the human shine in their ever-present assertions and demands. In soulful aging, one is lifted out of human weaknesses and given gratuitous dignity as a creature amongst all, connected to some eternal unfolding creative purpose and having meaning implicitly by being alive. Our infinite smallness and value are constant strivings in our being.

God and the Skater 1979

My mother stood in the pavilion
Watching over me as I skated
I loved my speed skates and each winter
I waited for the ideal idea on the lake.
This year it would be different
Amidst the months of uncertainty and fear I chose to skate
It was dark
The sun was fading
And few skaters remained on the now quiet ice
The snow glimmered in the long rays of light
And the Moon shone clear and proud
Silence stood around, as I glided in the rhythm of my skate
Each glide seemed perfect as the crisp ice grated and cut below the surface
I was being held in the love, hope and steadfast support of my mother
And the infinite grace of God
I felt held by some invisible peace and perfection on this high
God spoke in the moon and the stars and the fresh cold air all around
Everything seemed all right now
Ne fear, no emotion, just the ease of skating in the light
I gained energy and courage in this moment of love

I returned to know this silence and peace
God had spoken to me, the skater.

Everything in life and experience gets reframed in a moment and lifted as a flow, a dance, a firework of divine consciousness. The reality of life that is so near, brutal, violent, dark, and de-spirited gets subdued and understood by the working out of an expanded consciousness. My adult self can now embrace the richness and numerous perspectives amongst siblings, and it is wondrous to hear stories told through so many lenses. Through sharing of story and perceptions, we have become more accepting and sensitive to the variable personalities and ways of interpretation. In truth we have become more kind and forgiving in our soulful aging.

In August of 2020, I enjoyed some time off after working as a spiritual health practitioner. I had relocated back to NB from Vancouver and was trying to pivot professionally, contemplating change in the middle of the Covid pandemic, the upheaval of normal life and our shifting expectations.

That summer, I had been invited by a cousin to her beach cottage in Nova Scotia. As a child of 12, I swam in those waters and ran to the beach with her and her brother and cousins. I was delighted with the plan to go down for a few days to catch up.

I had a scheduled mammogram after discovering a questionable nodule. The mammogram ended up involving further tests and the radiologist offered to do an ultrasound and biopsy that afternoon. I agreed, feeling the urgency of her offer.

After the biopsy that afternoon I still wanted to take the drive to see my cousin. I had called her; cried some and then said I would still try to make it down for a visit. I stuffed my bra with the cold compresses provided and left in a race for NS. While there we did all the beautiful things typical of a cottage stay; we talked, ate crab, had some drinks, swam in the ocean, walked in the quiet tree-laden paths in the cooler summer shelter and shared the joy of her growing pre-teen son and welcomed her close friends that visited.

The news came back weeks later that I had HER2 estrogen and progesterone positive tumor in my right breast. That day, I was driving an older tennis buddy for a coffee and chat. We pulled over when the call came. I am sure he felt the emotion and tenor of my voice as I wrote down the news scratching out the words and missing some content as the brain sped through thoughts and emotions and tried to focus on the diagnosis. I kept that scratched piece of paper with the words, lines, and circles.

I was thankful that my sisters tried to encourage me to stay positive before the call. But I knew from the radiologist's words and approach, the final news would not be good.

We stopped for lunch. I could not focus on my friend nor on my meal and paused to send an email to my eldest sister. My eldest sister had the knack of being able to hold emotions in one of compassion, care and understanding. She did that for me, that day. She listened and she gave back words of love.

I could not cry with my friend. We just didn't have that kind of relationship. But he understood my fears and sympathized. He was present for me, and I knew that.

What is ironic is that my health was generally excellent other than the newly diagnosed cancer. I have low blood pressure, no diabetes, I am active physically and took only Thyroid medication (replacement for a Thyroid removed because of cancer in 1988). I enjoy a vibrant, dynamic, active, and beautiful life .... taking part-time philosophy courses from Dominican University College for fun, traveling, playing tennis in the summer, skating in the winter, honoring time with my adult children and visiting my sisters back and forth across provinces. I never had colds and didn't have covid throughout the two years of its threat. I had a little more weight on, but always enjoyed a primarily vegetarian lifestyle with an occasional dairy or sweet treat. But here was cancer looming over my life, yet again.

Within the month I was scheduled for surgery. My third eldest sister came down from Ottawa and we enjoyed a few days at a local downtown hotel as I recovered. The lumpectomy was precarious as one didn't know if a mastectomy might be required or if lymph nodes were involved. There were moments of care from my sister, son and daughter that helped to ease it all. My son dropped by before the night of the surgery with pizza (though I could not indulge) and my daughter dropped a vaporizer with fragrant oils, for the recovery. Two other siblings traveled up to visit and the next day we were having a seafood meal in a local restaurant. All these diversions and indulgences helped to just get me through any discomfort. The presence of my sisters made me present. The kindness and care surrounded me and cushioned the uncertainties.

I would hear after the surgery that they didn't get the margins of the tumor and there was an invasion of the tumor cells in the breast tissue, but no lymph nodes involved. I would unknowingly be in hospital for surgery for margins the following month. After the surgery, my oncologist who I have known for 40 years; and who is always kind and direct seemed to be hedging about some uncertainty. Eventually after further time and consultation, she advised a double mastectomy with no chemo or radiation. Five months after the initial diagnosis, I had a double mastectomy.

There were so many emotions involved in this journey. But the hardest emotion or period was waiting for word or confirmation of the next step. What was most helpful in recovery was the constant care of family. I am without a partner so my siblings assumed the responsibility for my care, collectively as sisters. But one sister carved out time and resources and very practical assistance as I recovered from my mastectomy. The impact of all this fear, anticipation, outcome, and recovery was taken incrementally with the presence of family. And how do you thank a sister for the very essence of care and companionship throughout such a multi-surgery year of trials and tribulations? The gift of her time and care permitted me to stand up sooner, to walk, to claim back my wellness and to push through my own boundaries.

One of my leanings as a patient was the constant desire to be further ahead in the recovery cycle. I tended to place unreasonable expectations on myself which ultimately created undue pressure and more duress. Once I accepted that it would take at least five weeks to heal the fourteen-inch scar and another five weeks to become active and able again, I judged less and accepted my curtailments more readily. One of those pushing moments involved skating on the frozen ice rink at Officers' Square in Fredericton. I was close to one-month post-surgery and wanted to skate. I had the skates sharpened and went to the rink. Ten minutes of skating in the brisk cold air was an emblem of my fortitude. Somehow we need these moments of breaking out into our humanity, expressing our needs, wants and desires and claiming the person we want to re-know and be.

Strangers reached out even when I didn't ask. Family reached out offering compassionate care even when I couldn't ask for help. My oncologist and specialists went beyond for me in acts of professionalism and compassion. Every single act of love matters in the recovery and restoration of the body, mind, and spirit.

The goodbye of a mastectomy -JR

A woman's breast and cancer
Brought together only ever in anguish
An encounter of misfortune and impending grief
A story of a breast turning on itself
Sometimes too late, gone too far
Shattered futures, facing determined hopes
Mustering inner capacities, quiet corners
And conversations with the One who can hear
Of loss and recovery
The diseased and disordered cancer invading
Or hiding in places beyond
Breast and nipple claimed,
Scarred and wrecked by disease
A common story in our time & living
One in eight women afflicted
The breast that comforted a child
Or pressed lovingly in a hug
There in affectionate sign
A gift of the body now adrift

Breast cancer at any age and stage
Affecting healthy body,
Encroaching & threatening
A radiologist, examinations & battery of scans
An oncologist delivering
The diagnosis
A surgeon removes tumour, treatment discussed
The patient and her tumult, ensue
Breasts will be severed
She accepts the radical
To be gone, breasts gone
Severed from cancer
For hope, for the future, for a promise
A leap of faith more than imagined
The body parted from cells, tissue and threat hanging over
The image flashes of past and future
As female, as woman, as mother and dreams of being grandmother
A breast does not make womanhood she cries
Nor a feminine nature need such for love she replies
Nor does diminish a flourishing life, she weakens
Though
Cancer threatens
And even foreshadows loss, mortality
Or plays out luck, fate and chance,
Or some play of admittance
A real scare, a real cost that must be paid
Lessons laid
A real risk of future disease quailing fears of ominous ends
Remember the start of needs versus wants
In middle school
At eleven, wanting breasts to be accepted
Her mother listened
Friends sporting theirs, boldly & boastfully
But she did not need breasts then
But found a bra
And those breasts eventually traveled
From university to career, to motherhood in play and recreation
From speed skating to field hockey to badminton courts, choirs, festivalsfestivals, and performances
They were visible and present in all personal transitions, successes growth and achievements
Sad moments and joyful moments
Those breasts there for a walk on the beach
Or on the tennis court competing
Sprouted fully after my child was born
They expressed my femininity and sexuality

Comfortably and easily
And sported a many t-shirt or summer dress on travels
As we took cross country explorations
As they settled well in motherhood, family and home
They were a perfect 32, and 34, then 36 and 38,
B, C and D and versions in-between
Funny to think about
Shapes and changes
All the sizes and forms they became, as I became
Journeying through transitions of life and hope,
they were there
Not one to flash a low cut dress or top
But they were there in pretty bra or basic black
They fit and were fine and I enjoyed them
Then
Yes, they were my friends
Never giving me trouble I was just lucky
Not too big and not too small
So I believed
And in the secret moments of life and intimacy
I knew they were an addition
But contemplating mastectomy
This invasive ductal carcinoma
Estrogen positive progesterone positive HER2 negative
Brings more invasive thoughts
I hold each breast as part of me, that made me whole
What or who would l be without them
Without my expressive nature
. . . it will be okay
Your self is not located in the external now
The voice of courage heard
Those breasts are not needed for inward and outward journeys you will take
Those Breasts can stay behind
The breast do not need to shelter others your love extends beyond
The breasts are traded for a longer life, pray
The breasts are left behind, diseased
Breasts traded for Time, more time
Breasts traded for Hope, the now
Breasts traded for Health, claim it
Breast traded for Happiness, delight in it
Breasts traded for Future, unstoppable
The breasts that cannot stop Desires
The breasts that cannot stop Dreams
Visions
Plans
I ready myself for surgery

The breasts will go away
And the Joy of life will remain
Scars will not hide
A need to accept and be accepted
The need to honor the light within and without
The desire for self-understanding and well-being
The setting of loving and caring above cosmetic acceptance
The seeking of integrity, authenticity & truth each day
A future above the some objective determinant of a female body
The priority of life, compassion and inner strength above digital standards
The importance of determination
Self-regard, will and clarity
Above short term claims, fames or banners
Fierce hope
Breasts be-gone
Women of all appearance
Fraternity of freedom,
No Breasts, no judgment,
No Breasts
Cancer free
Breast free
Embrace all who much take this journey of hope
Name oncologist, surgeon, nurse, or doctor that help women and men move forward
Practice kindness to other women on their journeys
Like the heart of a mother
That listened, wisely
I did not need breasts, nor do I now
Breast or No Breast I am free to be
Cancer-freed

Where am I now in the midst of this breast cancer journey? When I awake each morning, I have a prayerful moment that says thank you to God for this day . . . I am here, I am ok, I am whole. And then I hesitate; "No you had Cancer" and then I respond as my mother would urge me to say "No you are ok, you are not Cancer"! And then I take back the day. For me, turning back the day means reclaiming qualities of a good life: in peace, beauty, calm, happiness, kindness, compassion, freedom, hope and resting in well-being. The resting may take the form of a deep breath, touching a flower or seeing the beauty of a candle or the cloud passing in the sky. It is catching oneself in that moment that will never be repeated quite the same. Each moment invites me into that fulness of hope and transcendent goodness.

We must take the physical and emotional/psychological steps to enable well-being. I remember my father not sympathizing or pampering me after a radiation treatment but rather expecting me out on the tennis courts to join my siblings in spring training. I remember my poor-me mood. But tennis, skating, walks, drives, eating, laughing, and living life makes all better. We must seek help from professionals if we cannot help ourselves. Once we are stable, the momentum of adding good to our day matters. Many cancer patients experience exhaustion; talking about it, thinking of it, ruminating over it, and the ongoing drain on the body, mind and spirit is so defeating. Cancer disrupts the body. The body needs tender help to bring it back during or after treatment. The therapeutic arts can heal spiritually too: listening to music you love, meditation, painting and drawing, creative coloring, learning dance, gardening, or growing herbs,

cooking, writing poetry or prose, journaling. yoga, tai chi, qigong, and natural health resources.

After earning a BBA and MA in Public Administration, I began working for a Hospice in my local community begun by the Radiation Oncologist that had treated me for Hodgkins. I became the Hospice coordinator of volunteers that served patients in the community and I knew that this role resonated with who I was and what I could offer. I eventually moved to adult education work with community college and with my partner provided support and accompaniment to adults and youth returning to employment and job training. Study was something I loved and a decade later I said yes to a move to Vancouver and enrolled in a Masters in Theological Studies. This degree provided the offer of a beautiful position as campus minister of young adults at a liberal arts university in NB and working with many wonderful priests and persons in a chapel community. Post this position, I took a Clinical Pastoral Education program that led to several new and interesting roles as Spiritual Health Practitioner in several local hospitals on the east and west coast.

Cancer means to me; "Run more furiously towards the light", because turning away we avoid being absorbed into the abyss. Each of us must break free from definitions, refusing to be defined by disease or even our fears and limitations. I have learned to be a gatekeeper for my emotions when thoughts are negative or repeated. Place your tender rooted self into the joys you hold, turn to what you value in life; in the relationships, in work you love and bring the optimism and hope each day brings despite real threat to life. Remember life and death are so inextricably linked every moment of every day. Strengthen your capacity to love. Propel yourself to live more of life now. Don't wait for cancer to speak louder than your joys or loves.

As soon as we think we have known ourselves or have understood life, we inevitably fail in the living. As soon as we define good and bad, we must ultimately concede our poverty in seeing and being in between definitions. Each human awakening is but a child's discovery. Our learning can lean on wisdoms we sense and know, aware of their liminality and our own ever widening life experience. The process of discovering the inner, takes a while; decades upon decades. There is awakening in our ageing, but we keep forgetting that self-referential truth is universal for all. When we rely on habitual or pre-scripted ways of being and acting, we knowingly imprison our inner being.

My radical experience of cancer is the nexus for my learning and re-learning on soulful aging. Cancer radically defined and redefined how I see life. The reality of death and the hope of life redirected and fixed a firm post on life. Illness shaped an overarching reminder and thrust within me to seize life, to honor life and treasure it moment to moment. For me, there has always been a desire to think and reflect on experience and to share insights in poem, prose, or photography. When I think of my life as one melody, it could be summed up as: joyful, creative, sensitive, spiritual, stubborn, persistent, independent, and expressive. Because of this sensitivity, I became aware of my capacity to come alongside another, in pain or in crisis and can empathize with another in their normal everyday struggles offering deep listening, compassionate care and presence to family, friends and strangers. I remember these gifts given to me in my own life and the people who were my life teachers, all helping to shape that sensitive child. "She is the shy one, number four" one who could learn how to care and help.

In soulful aging there is a sense of receiving one's self in some utter nakedness and simplicity, attuned to the transcendent whispers of joy, the interior movements from moment to moment. We, in soulfulness, seek to attune an ear to hear so finely, see so deeply, look so curiously, with courage to redress our missteps and failures and falls. My first year of university as a young adult was the year of Cancer. I moved from science classes to business courses but what mostly attracted me were the philosophy courses that would permit me to ask Why? That question would never be answered and cannot be, but it is the summary of life and its immense mystery. For me Cancer would be seen as a gift; beauty, strangers and friendship, community encircling and spirit shining amidst suffering, fear, pain and uncertainty.

Soulful aging comes out of such a life embedded in community, love and endurance and tested by multiple cancer experiences. I love the beauty of the birch tree. My mother used to peel the bark and shape it into canoes for her maple fudge and divinity fudge which would be sent to school bazaars. The birch bark serves as a metaphor for life lived in this extended family. Deep roots of family values and companionship provided nourishment and stability. The roots reach out and even intertwine with fellow trees supporting and sharing nutrients as do my family. The growth of the tree in clusters broadens its resiliency. And the tree shows the challenging times and bad times of duress. The tree must reach beyond its environment. Our lives too are strengthened by growing our capacities and refining our emotional and adaptive capabilities. The tree does not always flower and does not always seed other trees. We too may or may not adapt and adjust to our changing and challenging pressures, weaknesses and environment.

Despite any spirituality, faith, or ethical framework we can be suddenly brought to our needy self in a moment. All the muscles of our spiritual life are suddenly weak or defunct. And within some formed and unexpected response we exhibit old patterns of justifying, explaining, manipulating, and defending our smallish identity in the world.

One way we are lifted up into an eternal moment is through the heart-to-heart sharing that can happen with friends, even strangers and sometimes even in our work. Certainly, for me in my work as a spiritual care practitioner, individuals have shared powerful, impactful stories with me that have moved my heart. When two hearts are connecting there is a resonance and power. There is a quiet joy of being understood and of understanding. Sometimes these vistas on our soul just come; they are not producible or replicable; they just emerge out of, spring up from and interrupt the ordinary. Somehow, we can read the integrity, the depth of feeling, the honesty in word and tone and we know that this human sharing is like the sunset, or the rose in full bloom or the tree in blossom; we know that human being can bring together exceptional understanding and growth and creativity that engenders new creative thoughts, movements, passions, and acts.

In my early work as a volunteer coordinator for a Hospice I had many spiritual teachers. I met patients who left an indelible impression on me. One was gaunt and in a gurney in the hall when I first greeted him. He was never able to leave the hospital and never made it to the community. Days before his death he had a smile, a warmth, as he reached out for my hand and said, "jump in here with me and we can chat". Perhaps another would have been offended .... but we laughed together. For me, his spirit was shining, and he said "I have had a wonderful life; and then proceeded to tell me why; he had married and loved, had family, played in a band, and had a faith that gave him consolation. He taught me about what kind of life I wanted!

Another lesson on soulful aging was at the threshold of his hospital door sitting dressed in civics and legs hanging over the side of the bed, after my knock on his door, greeting me effusively ""Come on in beautiful". I proceeded to provide the information on the palliative community support, and he proceeded to share that he was blind. I do not remember more than this brief moment but in that moment, this stranger taught me about my own expectations; what I see is not what is, what I know is not always true and he welcomed me, brought me into his space so abundantly through his bright affirming light.

I was learning in a new way about life and death and the liminal moments in life where life feels big. Another brief interaction occurred when I met a patient, a little woman lying in her bed with many pillows framing her small head of white hair. I do not remember the words she spoke, but I remember the light she had, I remember learning that a person who is sick or palliative can do so much. Here she was with me and able to share her light, to make me feel the warmth and beauty of that light and to make me know that she was still touching souls even in her palliative state. That was a powerful lesson; that we do not have to do in life, actions are not the only measurement of doing, measurable outcomes come from within, from the spirit. How do we affect another?

One young man that I visited was in a rural community. I traveled there by care, parked and then waited. He had several dogs in the yard, but they were tied up. I approached the door hesitantly. I was greeted by a man in his mid-thirties, who was married but dealing with a palliative diagnosis. He was angry about the illness. I remember feeling sorrow for him and wanting life for him. A volunteer would have been assigned to this patient. Weeks passed and I knew he was now in the palliative unit at the hospital. I went to see him. And he was completely transformed. This angry young man was gone and there was a resigned peaceful man before me; it was incredulous. I could hardly process this change. And he said, "Do you see the sky, see how easily the plane is going through the clouds". I knew what he was saying. I was amazed at the transformation in his spirit and this learning had a profound impact on me. I left . . . .and had a good cry in the hospital chapel. I was happy that he was in this "place" of acceptance and that the anger had turned to peace. This was almost a miraculous thing for me, the change, and the beauty of this man. I also learned about journeying with someone and how the change sometimes is subtle or the transformation in our spirit can be clear, powerful, and impactful. I thought it unjust that he would die so soon, in the midst of life, but here before me was a man who had integrated this prognosis and accepted his fate.

I have always been amazed by the resiliency of elders especially when they live to a very senior age. One woman, a beloved friend, has belied ageism. In her early nineties she could be seen walking uphill smartly dressed in slacks and a jacket with hair styled and earrings hanging. But it is her stated vocation that is most interesting and enlightening. She believes it to be "living the art of life". As an artist she has painted and created, had family and grandchildren and created a household, but her own creative art she believes is "how" she lives her life. That life is expressive, deep, connecting and going out from her home into the lives, coffee shops, book groups, festive celebrations, lectures, caring for others through word, small acts of kindness and recognition of another human being. She loves bouquets and picking flowers at the shore and her home is a testimony to a well lived life; art, weathered favorite things, the ritual of lighting a candle and stocking the fireplace to create a hearth where company connection and creative conversation can thrive. She is prepared to take risks, to stand in her own integrity and truths, to learn and to understand from different generations, and to review and muse on her life and its significant signposts. Truly she is a lesson in aging.

For me encounters with people who are aware of their spirit is a thrill and offers such learning and miraculous moments. Today I went to the gym. It is a practice that I recently returned to this year after being absent for six years. And a young woman was at the desk. She is an immigrant from Afghanistan. She smiles and greets people with warmth and beauty. She said to me that she needs to work on her English but I said, "Well that will happen but in the meantime you communicate beautifully with all who you greet at the welcome desk with your smile". How can I affirm and honor another's spirit? When can I encourage and affirm another on their path? Beauty lies in so many places and we should stop to see it.

These memories of beauty, fullness, largeness add such vitality to life. I have experienced the compassion of others. I honor so many persons of compassion who acknowledge the beauty and gift of another's soul. I treasure the goodness of health professionals who really seek to be human and life-giving in their work. I am indebted to the many ways people carry my burden and unburden life for me, thank you, thank you, thank you loved ones and special angels who have helped in ways that I could not fathom. I have received so much abundance which permits me to be Well.

All life is seen as imbued with divinity and sacredness. Each particularity as it shifts and changes expresses and grows the ultimate expression and our understanding of the universal. We are but instances of this incredible unfolding creation. But let us not diminish the greatness of incredibleness of each instance, each life form and each moment of each radiance.

In the twinkling of an eye

Sarah Robinson Flick

ABSTRACT
This essay explores the impact of inevitable uncertainty during the aging process and explores the effects of uncertainty on our spiritual experience during our elder years. It offers the role of touchstones as reminders of all that we have loved and posits that as long as we have breath, our deepest desires enfold us in our own spiritual growth. By deepening and broadening our understanding of desire, we can experience our individual spiritual growth as the product of love and compassion.

> "Listen, I will tell you a mystery! We will not all die, but we will all be changed, in a moment, in the twinkling of an eye, at the last trumpet. For the trumpet will sound, and the dead will be raised imperishable, and we will be changed" (1 Corinthians, Chapter 15: Verses 51-52, New Testament, New Revised Standard Version).

Soulful aging. My first thoughts about aging, both my own thoughts and memories of others' thoughts that have been shared with me, are a bubbling stewpot filled with expectations, hopes, dreams, fears, anxiety, dread, disgust, avoidance, escape, denial, and mean jokes. Sprinkled with idealization and skeptical hopes for some influence, some autonomy that we might be able to exert, some choice that we might surely be able to make. I worked for many years as a child psychiatrist. My choice of subspecialty was deliberate and intentional. I love children and young people. As the oldest of four daughters, my young world was most dramatically rocked by the arrival of my sister, and then the next sister, and then the youngest sister. Eight years of an ever-evolving family of origin brought me to enjoy babies, toddlers, and children as they grew. Today there is a shortage of child psychiatrists. There is also a shortage of geriatric psychiatrists. And somehow all the babies and children and adolescents I have known, patients and family and friends and those I see on the airplane or in the grocery store, all of us are now actually aging. I am about to enter my eighth decade, and that hardly even seems real. But it is, and so I think more and more now not as a psychiatrist (of any specialty), but as someone looking at a road less traveled. A road available only to those who live long enough to arrive there. Aging is real and we are doing it. I can attest that it is already soulful for me. But maybe not so much in the ways I have always anticipated.

I am neither a scripture scholar nor a music expert. Like much of life, both scripture and music have found their way to me experientially, much like aging has found its way to me experientially. The passage from 1 Corinthians referenced above is woven into the well-loved Handel's Messiah oratorio. When we were young children, my father would play the entirety of the record albums of Handel's Messiah very early on Sunday mornings. We would awaken to this music and these words embedded in this amazing oratorio. Somehow, I came to know the entire piece. I went to many concerts where Handel's Messiah was performed. I stood up with the audience at the magnificent Hallelujah Chorus, stunned by the participation. This section, and the piece that follows, "The Trumpet Shall Sound," were played at my beloved uncle's funeral. I was not there, but my father was, and he was quick to tell me that this was part of the music played at that service. I love all of Handel's Messiah, not because I had to learn it in school or perform it, but because it was woven into the fabric of my everyday and longitudinal life. The words that first caught me, and that have remained with me primarily, are "in the twinkling of an eye" (1 Cor. 15: 51–52 NRSV). I remember very early as a young child that these words somehow reminded me of Tinkerbell in Peter Pan, another early musical experience. "in the twinkling of an eye" (Ibid.) mingled with Tinkerbell and Neverland and I suppose that it still does in many ways. I find the common ground here to be one of our lesser liked experiences, that of uncertainty.

The one thing about soulful aging that I experience as certain (so far) is uncertainty itself. Uncertainty may be, in many ways, one of our most challenging landscapes. As children, we might enjoy fantasy, fairy tales, imaginative play, model trains, stuffed animals, and dolls. We are engaged, nurtured, and comforted by "real" things and also by "unreal" things. The distinction does not seem to impact the outcome here as our imagination grows and becomes richer and helps us understand the world around us. Soon enough, we learn that some things are real, and others are not. We encounter a diversity of beliefs, of opinions, of expectations, of transactional relationships. If we are lucky, we may have opportunities for creativity. With time and aging, we find ourselves in a world fashioned by data and media and crises of many kinds. Certainty becomes harder to find and harder to achieve, and yet it remains our metric of choice in many arenas. Even religion that asks us to consider and adopt the "certainty" of faith knows now that a pandemic can appear, and church services can be canceled for many months. Weddings and funerals might have to be changed, delayed, or canceled and at the very time that we need most to be together with loved ones. We might cling to "certainty" and that can be our choice. The reality of uncertainty is becoming clearer to me as my aging years appear. The world around me feels very uncertain in many ways. It might just be my perception, but it might not be. "In the twinkling of an eye" (Ibid.) we have learned of natural disasters, of inhumanity on the streets and in our institutions, and of sudden devastating loss. The same words that St. Paul and Handel use to reference eternity also signal impermanence and unexpected instantaneous change to me. Our world feels uncertain now and maybe it always has.

Aging, as I have observed in loved ones, and now as I have begun and continue to experience it myself, makes uncertainty the name of the game. Each of us will experience aging differently and on different days at different times. We have learned about some of the hallmarks of aging and what to expect broadly if we live long enough to literally age. We all travel towards death and some reach it much much sooner than others. Some of us live for what we call "a very long time." It is clear to me that time is more relative now than ever before. I'm not sure how much this matters or even if it does matter, but it makes me curious. And that is important. Our curiosity is important. Our curiosity, if we are open to it, can be an antidote to our anxiety. When I hear the words "in the twinkling of an eye" (Ibid.) I think of rapid change. My anxiety is provoked by rapid change, and "in the twinkling of an eye" (Ibid.) makes me curious. What does the twinkling of an eye look like? How long does it really take? Whose eye is twinkling? Is it beautiful and filled with light? Curiosity can mediate and even displace anxiety. Uncertainty might lead to anxiety and curiosity awakens our imagination, the same imagination that we found ourselves at play in as small children who were unworried about "real and unreal." Curiosity can be soulful when it expands our landscape, helps us find light, facilitates our sight of what is beyond "real," inspires hope.

Uncertainty is a common ground of aging. Soulful aging is an embodiment of our human experience of uncertainty. There is so much that we don't know, so much that we can't know. Some of the most tender moments of practicing medicine are the conversations about prognosis, about what is going to happen and what the outcome will be. We have these conversations with others as children, as parents, as siblings, as friends, as lovers. When a patient looks in our eyes, when a loved one looks in our eyes and asks, "what's happening to me?" what do we say? How do we answer? What answer are we listening for when we ask our own questions? Often, there may be predictable events about to happen, but, even as someone is dying, most of us cannot know for sure the time and the place. We can try to anticipate all that we can. A great deal of information is available about the dying process itself and professionals such as hospice providers and palliative care professionals can be very helpful. And sometimes people just do not wake up. There is an automobile accident. Someone is caught in a crossfire on a street or in a grocery store or in a church or in a school or at an airport. Timelines are all over the place. A common denominator is uncertainty. Not only about death but also aging itself whenever it begins to appear in our experience. We can practice healthy behaviors and early intervention (if we are fortunate enough to have access to healthcare) and even be grateful for favorable genetics. All of these are important ways to support ourselves. We still cannot know for sure either what will happen to us or what the outcome will be. This is somewhat true for all our lives, but as we age, these questions become highlighted for many of us. We can pretend otherwise, but this uncertainty of aging reaches new existential meaning for us, and we experience it on multiple levels within ourselves. Whether we find refuge in denial or are directly involved in anticipatory or current losses, our bodies tell us that there is less time ahead of us than behind us. We wonder how to make "the best" of whatever time we have left. This is hard when we might not know how much time or what kind of time we have left. Uncertainty takes its place at our table, and we wonder what direction to choose as we begin to welcome this visitor.

Sometimes we carry something with us throughout our lives. It might be an image of our childhood home. It might be a song. It might be a favorite book or movie, and it might be a dream, a fantasy, or a memory, a moment of love. These touchstones can both comfort and challenge us. They can remind us of who we are. A wedding ring or a high school or college class ring are signals to the world around us and to ourselves of who we are. When we find ourselves in uncertainty, a touchstone can reorient us to what we do know. If uncertainty is in fact a certainty of aging, touchstones from throughout our lives can accompany us into and through uncertainty, reminding us of who we are. Some touchstones are objects and some live inside us. A touchstone can remind us to be curious. "In the twinkling of an eye" (Ibid.) reminds me of love. It reminds me of being very young. It reminds me of the beauty of music. I have always hoped that the twinkling of an eye would be accompanied by light, like a sparkler or a birthday cake candle. I have loved these words since I was a young child. I have learned that when rapid change is coming, comes, has come, I can look for the light. It might be a horrible heartbreaking rapid change, and one thing I know I can do is to look for the light. It has never failed me. Even if it is just one star in the sky or a single night light, it has helped me to look for and find and even create light with a flashlight and to know that whatever happens I will still see light as long as I have sight, and I can see light in my imagination as long as I live. It does not mean that rapid change is good (although it could be) and it does mean that I can look for and see myself in the light. I can live in uncertainty by the light of a candle, by the light in my beloved's eyes.

For me, aging at its bedrock signals uncertainty. Indefinite in time and space and quality of life kind of uncertainty. The only desires that I am sure about for my own aging are that I might suffer as little as possible, that I be able to read as long as possible, that I can hear music as long as possible, that I can be with my loved ones as long as possible (and that they too suffer as little as possible as I age and die), and that I can be in nature as long as possible. And access to ice cream, cheese, and chocolate if I had one more wish. And, if I had yet one more wish, I would want to carry "in the twinkling of an eye" (Ibid.) as my touchstone. It means so much to me. I write this still in my 60's and so I would also reserve the right to change my mind and to laugh at the certainty of uncertainty.

Aging does happen if we are lucky. I come from a family lineage of some young deaths and a few rare extraordinary long-lived relatives whose legends I learned many years ago. Uncertainty is a spiritual practice. Touchstones are a spiritual practice. Being ourselves authentically is one of the most advanced spiritual practices I know. I pray that my own path is marked by curiosity in the face of uncertainty, touchstones that remind me of love, and the courage and grace to be myself. This would be soulful aging for me. I am open to changing my mind and my other prayer, my deepest one of all, is that I will always look for the light and know that love always remains.

I wish for all of humanity to help each other to suffer as little as possible. I wish that soulful aging would be accessible to each of us in our own path, to all of us in our own paths. I wish that each of us may know our own desires and that we can together support each other to create ways to fulfill our desires. May soulful aging become for us a path of beauty, a path of tenderness, a path of comfort with releasing certainty, and a path of peace for us, for our loved ones, for common humanity. May soulful aging become our sacrament. May we, may all of us, always look for the light and may we all know forever that love always remains.

Disclosure statement

No potential conflict of interest was reported by the author.

ORCID

Sarah Robinson Flick http://orcid.org/0009-0009-4087-0784

Reference

1 Corinthians Chapter 15 Verses 51-52 NRSV.

The poetics of soulful aging

Braveheart Gillani

ABSTRACT

Soulful aging is a process of adding meaning to each part of the aging process. In order to navigate the wilderness of soulful aging, this essay seeks wisdom from ancient and contemporary sages, poets, philosophers, and analysts- weaving modern practices of mindful living and meaning creation with age old and sanctified notions of attaining wisdom. The author provides three axis of contemplation and paradigms to engage with while navigating soulful aging (1) Decolonizing Aging (2) Queering Aging and (3) Befriending aging.

Introduction

What is soulful aging in the modern age-a time which balks at beliefs about the soul and maligns aging? When invited to contribute to the special issue titled "soulful aging," I was plagued by questions for weeks. I wondered, can one who is not yet considered "aged" (I am in my mid-thirties) by norms of society develop a meaningful conversation around soulful aging? And can the writing be more than an intellectual exegesis of definitions and declarations- removing the soul itself from the writing and, therefore, from soulful aging? Can I instead hold space for an anthem of hope around the process of soulful aging? Can I seek wisdom across intellectual, spiritual, and poetic dimensions and chisel out some words to give myself and others handles to grasp while navigating the storms of life? Holding both the doubts and fears in trembling hands, I explore dimensions and poetics of soulful aging- within literature (both academic and not), grey literature, poetry, and myself.

All knowledge is developed within relationships (Kalanithi, 2020, T Black, personal communication, 6/12/2021). In fact, knowledge which does not flow for community and conversation is disembodied (Hope, 2005). It may contain facts but lacks the penetration required for wisdom and integration. For this manuscript, I talked to mentors (both who know me and have personal relationships with me, and authors who do not personally know me but have mentored me across my life), students, friends, community members and neighbors. I sought perspectives from academics and blue collared friends (plumbers, carpenters and roofers), individuals from the United States, Europe and Asia, people strictly within the cis-hetero-patriarchal norms and those who are not represented by any existing labels. I chatted with retired folks along with those at the cusp of youth, those who are highly valued by society and those struggling with addictions. I sought answers in monotheistic and polytheistic epistles, in the songs of the sages and flippant banters at barber shops, within poetry and prose, so-called self-help books and gems forgotten by the internet age, social media, AI chatbots and everything in between. I profess to. And finally, I sought wisdom from the Divine through meditation and communion with the more-than-human world (Kinship, 2022). This manuscript is interspersed with field notes from my personal journals- reflexive moments concerning aging, growth, and transitions within age, gender, and hopefully soulfulness. They represent moments of extreme dissonance, (dis)embodiment, acknowledgement, or sheer confusion- all of which are parts of soulful aging.

This essay is more a prayer of desperation (which Rumi reminds us all prayers are) (Rumī & Barks, Jalāl Al-Dīn & Barks, 2003) than a typical research article. The quest is not to pursue answers but to "love the questions now and then gradually, without noticing, live into the answers some distant day" (Rilke, 2021). So as with all quests, I start this manuscript with a prayer of imperfection, growth, and meaning.

> So let us pick up the stones over which we stumble, friends, and build altars. Let us listen to the sound of breath in our bodies. Let us listen to the sounds of our own voices, of our own names, of our own fears. Let's claw ourselves out from the graves we've dug. Let's lick the earth from our fingers. Let us look up and out and around. The world is big and wide and wild and wonderful and wicked, and our lives are murky, magnificent, malleable, and full of meaning. Oremus. Let us pray. (O'tuama, 2021)

The author's positionality is critical, especially while dwelling on a notion as personal and yet universal as spiritual aging. I hold the vantage point of one approaching the threshold of my second half of life (Hollis, 2006)- hoping to find and create meaning. As the Jungian mastermind, James Hollis, states, "The goal of the second half of life, if summed up, is not goals but meaning." (Hollis, 2006) A millennial by age, my daily communication is steeped in gifs, googling terms, AI, emails, tweets and memes. Like others, chronological age is not the only dimension I operate in. I identify as a queer, immigrant, intersectional scholar of color. I also identify as an American, a Pakistani, a student, a friend, a community member and a dog host (I detest the term "owner"), all of which I hold with equitable amounts of honor and humility. I am a transgender man, undergoing gender-affirming care through the medical model. Gender affirming care in my middle age has generously afforded me the vantage point to see and be reflexive about a fast-forwarded process of my physical aging process manifesting my gender identity. Some of my reflections within this manuscript come from the locale of "crossing" genders while aging- hence aging simultaneously in multiple dimensions. This is a dynamic process, one which has challenged my notions of love and self- acceptance to the core. I am not unique in this experience- it is one frequently mentioned within the transgender community. Eli Clare mentions this as "Our body-minds tumble, shift, ease their way through space and time, never static. Gender transition in its many forms is simply another kind of motion. I lived in a body-mind assigned female at birth and made peace with it But uncovering my desire to transition – challenged everything I thought I knew about self-acceptance and love (Clare, 2017)."

Above all, I acknowledge being a product of my time- an intersectional human surviving the Anthropocene and being a witness to the planet's murder by human extractivist greed.

The purpose of this manuscript is to build a monument of wisdom and reflections for the beloved readers and my future Self, a metaphorical place to return to, build with and renovate when deeper truths are identified. I begin with the concept of soulful aging and clarify how it is distinguished from the general aging process. I explore the overlapping constructs of time and aging from various intentionally meandering directions with direct implications for soulfulness. Finally, I provide three large invitational paradigms for soulful aging- decolonizing aging, queering aging, and finally, affective aging. These ruminations are intentionally slanted towards queerness as a reclaimed term with the explicit agenda of highlighting and elevating queerly embodied ways of theorizing during an intentional, soulful aging process. For this manuscript, I use the term queer, which is inclusive of all individuals who desire to be included and do not fit cis-hetero-patriarchal youth-centric societal norms. I take a stand for an explicitly positive leaning towards soulful aging- wishing it possible for all who desire it. Holding space for a soulful global future is in itself a queer act of resistance to the rampant neo-liberal apathy prevalent within the society.

Soulful aging- what is it?

The quest for soulful aging

> *"Is there a way you can look any older? How are you going to manage a group of grown men if you look so young. Maybe put some lipstick or mascara on" said Bob while assigning a new project to me. I looked at him, deeply exhausted and offended. This is the third time this week my "childish look" has appeared as a problem for the management to solve. I shrug his suggestion off nonchalantly. I don't know how to tell him- if the choice is to look like a child or like a woman, I choose the former"[Stated to me by an international Oilfield Executive as I prepare to lead a group of three hundred plus men on an offshore oil rig in the Gulf of Mexico in a multimillion dollar project execution] Gillani 4/13/2016*

Aging has not always been embraced in Western societies as a positive attribute. A harbinger of death that symbolizes ultimate failure in modern capitalism, aging often has channeled notions of fear within communities. With the advent of the average human life span increasing significantly post-1960s as per the latest census reports, the stigma around aging has somewhat decreased (Emlet, 2016). Even though the quest for attaining the fountain of youth and immortality remains grounded in the human psyche, the call for living soulful and grounded adult lives retains its importance and place within human consciousness (Parker, 2022).

Even though the terms spiritual aging and soulful aging are used interchangeably within the literature, I offer slight distinctions between them. Soulful aging is the larger construct focusing on the emotional, psychological and spiritual aspects of aging (Simmons & Wilson, 2001). It focuses on the emotional and personal aspects of an individual's life as they progress in age and are driven away from ego-centric activities toward developing a sense of meaning and purpose in life. On the other hand, spiritual aging tends to focus more specifically on the spiritual or religious aspects of aging (Bianchi, 2011). It may involve exploring spiritual practices and traditions, deepening one's connection to a higher power or sense of spirituality, and seeking non-material contributions. Ultimately, spiritual aging may be seen as a sub-set of soulful aging, a time for integration and wholeness.

> *In a positive sense, aging becomes a time for visiting the temple of your memory and integrating your life ... Sometimes difficulty is the greatest friend of the soul.* (O'donohue, 1998)

Soulful aging refers to the process of growing and evolving as a person, both spiritually and emotionally, as we step forward in chronological age (Smart, 2021). It involves cultivating a sense of purpose and meaning in life, developing a deeper understanding of ourselves and our place in the world, and growing in our relationships with others. Soulful aging includes the development and embodiment of wisdom. Smart (2021) identifies the conglomerate construct of wisdom as consisting of the five features of (1) critical life experiences, (2) emotional regulation, (3) reminiscence/reflectiveness, (4) openness to experience and (5) humor (Smart, 2021). Soulful aging integrates wisdom in both short and long-term praxis- often to the chagrin of normative society. Societal appeasement is not included in the curricula of soulful aging. James Hollis clarified this as "We are not here to fit in, be well balanced, or provide example for others. We are here to be eccentric, different, perhaps strange, perhaps merely to add our small piece, our little clunky, chunky selves, to the great mosaic of being. As the gods intended, we are here to become more and more ourselves" (Hollis, 2010). Hence a potential index of soulful aging might be a conscious and careful (re)becoming of our own unique Self(ves) despite resistance from the society.

Necessary costs of soulful aging

> *"She lost connection to her entire family and community. They disowned her, labeled her as crazy and a heretic and discredited her. She lived through hell- homelessness- HIV. And look at her now! She has lost all her contemporary trans women- every single one of them. To AIDS, homicide, poverty . . . .all symptoms of transphobia. And yet, there is such joy in her! She is my hero(ine). [Name redacted] is saving the lives of so many simply by living her authentic life" [written about a 55 year old transwoman, the oldest "alive and out" trans women of color visible within the LGBTQ community in a midsized midwestern town after having a conversation with her] Gillani 6/12/2020*

Soulful aging, as the beloved reader may have deciphered already, involves a deep commitment to personal growth and self-awareness- often at the cost of looking good or "normal" to society. The resistance to aligning with the status quo exists across one's life course, and the challenge to become more of the true Self and resist becoming another consumer in a capitalistic society is immense (Albinsson & Yasanthi Perera, 2012). Resistance, whether from the inner Self or the society as one chooses to "mature" or "soulfully age," exists across the literature. Whether one uses the metaphor of the "hero's journey" (Campbell, 2020) or notions of post-traumatic growth (Kadri et al., 2022), it is clear that certain adversity levels within adulthood initiate growth and maturity. Soulful aging asks individuals not to dismiss adversity but to engage it. The great sage M. Scott Peck explains this: "Once we truly know that life is difficult – once we truly understand and accept it – then life is no longer difficult. Because once it is accepted, the fact that life is difficult no longer matters" (Peck, 2008).

The task of soulful aging is to get closer and closer to the authentic Self. Self-becoming is a long and lonely journey. This is expressed by James Hollis as "so, then, now you know your task: to become what the gods want, not what your parents want, not what your tribe wants, but what the gods want, and what your psyche will support if consciousness so directs." The question of how one knows what one "wants" within the paradigm of soulful aging appears. I offer that the "Want" of the higher Self within soulful aging is distinct from the wants, the greeds, lusts, desires and yearning for material or status-based wealth- all of which are seeded by ego and insecurity. This "Want" of the higher self which is the propeller for soulful aging is one which promotes community well-being. Community includes one and all, provides societal justice and is designed in service of the ancestors and the legacy rather than for one's individual temporal success.

No simple answers

> *"She asked me how I am going to "come-out" to everyone. I don't know. I still don't. It is question I have been grappling with all my life, and perhaps will continue doing so for the rest of it. Why is gender identity or sexuality so important to "come out" about- as compared to other facets of a soul? I continue coming out to myself and the world daily- about new interests, loves, desires and fears. The demand for disclosure is suffocating, but at the right time- disclosure- regardless of its reception is liberating" [when "coming out" about my gender identity to a decade long friend] Gillani 1/12/2021*

There is no clear measurement tool or strategy for soulful aging. Sages and guides from across the ages have presented solutions that may or may not work for individuals. Soulful aging often involves exploring spiritual practices and traditions that can help the practitioner connect with a more profound sense of meaning and purpose. Identifying philosophies, guides, and strategies that help individuals navigate the murky waters of the time are salient features of soulful aging, as is a sense of letting go of certain ego-driven desires. The individual is conflicted between the demands of the gods (career, fame, family, progress) and the demands of the Higher Self (belonging, love, embodiment, community etc.).

> *I want to know if you are prepared to live in the world with its harsh need to change you. If you can look back with firm eyes saying this is where I stand. . . . .It is said in that field embrace, even the gods speak of God* (Whyte, 1999)

Each chunk of time is murky for the soul, for it is the ego that tends to find clear-cut and often incorrect easy answers to questions that have "no right to go away (Whyte, 2011a). The modern sage David Whyte identifies these as those questions which shape our future self(ves) and which compel us (consciously or unconsciously) to go beyond our current standards of generosity and courage (Whyte, 2011b).

The call for creating meaning and finding ways to contribute to the larger collective may also be seen as a part of soulful aging. It must be reiterated that soulful aging may not always be a function of chronological age and is associated with one's inner life. Ultimately, I humbly offer that the driver for soulful aging is individuation or wholeness, which may promote community well-being, often at the expense of the individual ego (Hollis, 2018).

Time and soulful aging- enmeshed companions

Does time always move at the same speed?

> *"Damn- you look like you grew five years in the last six months," said my friend David as I reconnected with him on zoom. We connect regularly, yet the pandemic, a busy semester, and various other commitments have kept us apart. He looks at my freshly bearded face, the new wrinkle lines, and is astounded. So am I. The algorithm on google photos no longer recognizes me as me!" [written a year into my gender transition]* Gillani, 7/1/2022

How does a society complicit in youth worshipping and desiring of immortality grapple with the obvious and explicit wear and tear of the body over time? Additionally, how does the aging community hold ideas of time without imbibing all conversations with a morbid sense of doom of loss with death? Concepts of time are ubiquitous in explorations of aging and gerontology. Time within its various understandings and uses, is a critical tool – helpful in thinking about notions around aging. The term aging implicitly indicates the passage of chronological time. Does chronological aging also encapsulate within itself soulful aging? If not, what are some places to create and practices to embody which may promote soulful aging along with chronological aging? Chronological aging stops for no one, but does the same statement apply to soulful aging? Many examples in the modern age point to the sad reality that in a society filled with unlimited distractions, soulful aging may stagnate without deliberate efforts, consciousness, and sagacious mentorship.

Gerontology as a field offers a protected space where essential conversations around different dimensions of aging can be explored. It enables us to think of time from various dimensions and explore how the aging population can be supported and simultaneously- how can the aging support society? Here, I am making a distinction between the terms "aging" and "aged." Aging refers to the ongoing chronological process of all beings and objects. The aged are those who are considered to be towards the later end of their aging journey. The concept of deep time might be helpful to consider that what humans consider as aging and aged are minuscule when considered within the larger epoch of time. Deep time can both render human life meaningless and create hope for planetary survival

> *For deep time is measured in units that humble the human instant: millennia, epochs and eons, instead of minutes, months and years. Deep time is kept by rock, ice, stalactites, seabed sediments and the drift of tectonic plates. Seen in deep time, things come alive that*

seemed inert. New responsibilities declare themselves. Ice breathes. Rock has tides. Mountains rise and fall. We live on a restless Earth. (Macfarlane, 2020)

Soulful aging as presence in kairos

The Greeks conceptualized time with two different words- Chronos and Kairos. Chronos, with the same roots as chronological and chronicle, refers to time measured by the calendar or clock. It is fleeting, always on the move, and a bully. Aging in Chronos is, unfortunately, often framed as losing power, agility, and memory. The aged individuals lose their virility, often strategies of building a legacy diminish, and are filled with the fear of death. However, there can be great solace within the shadows of stepping away from a glamorized youth. John O Donohue, the beloved Irish priest, noted, "aging is not merely about the body losing its poise, strength, and self-trust. Aging also makes you aware of the sacred circle that shelters your life. Within the harvest circle, you can gather lost moments and experiences, bring them together, and hold them as one ... Aging can be a time of great strength, poise, and confidence." (O'donohue, 2005) Holding the notions of soulful and graceful aging, empowerment, and deep time, one comes to recognize as Robert McFarlane does that "We are tiny (and powerful) beings, fleeting as mayflies, in deep time's fullness" (Macfarlane, 2020).

To get a deeper understanding of Soulful Aging, the reader is invited to step away from Chronos and delve into what the Greek identified as "Kairos." In ancient Greek literature, Kairos often referred to the right or opportune moment for taking action, and it was often depicted as a personified figure holding a pair of scales (Boschung, 2013). The idea was that Kairos was a fleeting moment that needed to be seized to achieve success or make the most of an opportunity. The tools for measuring Kairos are more ephemeral- a laugh, a glimpse of someone's smile, a meaningful conversation. It is an experience of timelessness and transcendence, where time seems to stop and flow simultaneously (Boschung, 2013).

> Yet the timeless in you is aware of life's timelessness,
>
> And knows that yesterday is but today's memory and tomorrow is today's dream.
>
> And that which sings and contemplates in you is still dwelling within the bounds of that
>
> first moment which scattered the stars into space. (Gibran, 2008)

The knowledge of time being condensed, the confirmation of the past, and the future being bound with meaning catalyzes soulful aging. It inspires us to honor each person regardless of chronological age- as that is but one way of measuring development. These realizations help individuals burdened by the mundane tasks of life to engage in non-transactional relational spaces. They birth friendships, mentorships, philanthropic gestures, and potentially love.

The audacity of acknowledging the simultaneously fleeting presence and abundance in the nature of time inspires gestures of magnanimity, kindness, and potentially the human capacity to grieve and embrace death.

> To make friends with the hours is to come to know all the hidden correspondences inside our own bodies that match the richness and movement of life (and death) we see around us. (Whyte, 2023)

Befriending time means changing our relationship to it, from a bully, captor or even an enemy to a collaborator and a beloved. Language and metaphor shift is essential for changing this relationship. Instead of "killing time", how can we embrace and delight in it? Instead of "time-blocking" (Newport, 2019),can we allow it to flow and be- and dance around it? Befriending time is about inviting Chronus, the Greek God of time in our lives rather than constantly slamming the door at his face. Chronus invites us to think about all of time as the "eternal present" where the past, present and future have no boundaries. Time can be visualized as amorphous rather than a solid- changing states guiding us at each moment towards a greater sense of transcendence rather than trapping us within narrower and narrower slivers of existence.

Personal authority, crossing thresholds, and vulnerability in soulful aging following the (inner) guide

> *Of course, I know this (gender) transition will cost me! I will be ostracized by many. And fetishized by others. It is just that not being my full self is costing me a whole lot more- it is costing me my desire to live. It is costing me being me.* I am ready to pay!
>
> *[stated during a conversation with my therapist where I talk about beginning my medical gender transition] Gillani 7/4/2021*

> Growing up spiritually means that we are asked to sort through the possibilities for ourselves, find what resonates for us, what is confirmed by our experience, not the consensus of others, and be willing to stand for what has proved true for us. For this reason, the twin tasks of finding personal authority and finding a mature spirituality are inextricably linked (Hollis, 2006).

Hence, soulful aging lies beyond integrating a mature spirituality and finding personal authority. There is an invitation to cross certain thresholds of immaturity (which is different from childishness) and find what poets have titled one's voice. This voice- recognized by poets and sages across the ages, invokes a greater sense of authority, self-recognition, self-forgiveness, celebration, and self-respect. In his poem "love after love," Derek Walcott identifies this voice of self-acceptance and love when he states, "you will love again the stranger who was yourself." (Walcott, 2011). This "stranger" enables the person to tread on the path of individuation, fully aware of the internal and external resistance and committed to following the invitation of the Higher Self. Mary Oliver, in "the journey," recalls this voice of knowing, which becomes the only one worthy of following (Oliver, 2020). Whether it is a voice one hears, or an inscription on one's soul, the poets speak of moments of awareness when they commit to more profound, more authentic ways of living (Whyte, 2019).

Are you really ready to lose it all?

> *"The cop looked at my license, then me, then the photo on the license again. His voice had a tinge of aggravation as he said, "and this is you?". I faked my coolest smile. "Yes officer – I said. Just a bad photo of me- and some facial hair". He shook his head and walked away after giving me a ticket. Is this humiliation worth it? Yes indeed." [written a little over a year into my gender transition after being stopped by the police] Gillani 5/3/2021*

With excruciating vulnerability and the sheer impossibility of knowing what lies beyond the thresholds of daily life, this voice helps folx transition- gender, role, life stage, or more- into more of themselves (Lindsay et al., 2021). These transitions don't stop until death (and we have no knowledge of them stopping even after death), the horizons shifting at each state but retaining their gravitas. No longer deterred by changes, there folx have the moral "audacity" to lead society into new horizons of meaning making and understanding.

"To find ourselves, we must first lose ourselves, and crossing any true threshold is a time of great vulnerability when we are most alive and most open to the world around us. It is the threshold between the familiar and the unknown, between the safe and the unsafe, between the known and the unknowable, and it is in these spaces that we find ourselves, our most vulnerable selves, and in that vulnerability, we find the greatest gifts." – Whyte, 2020

Another aspect of claiming personal authority during soulful aging is claiming one's simultaneous authority and complete vulnerability and helplessness around time itself.!

> Time is a river which sweeps me along, but I am the river; it is a tiger which destroys me, but I am the tiger; it is a fire which consumes me, but I am the fire. (Borges et al., 2007)

Bereft of Time

> *"I think you think too much. You give too many F###. Just stop caring man. Don't you just want to party and hang out? Let me buy you a drink"[Reaction of a friend when I "came out" to him] Gillani 8/1/2020*

For the modern person striving towards soulful aging, wrestling one's time back from the multitudes of distractions is a feat to be contended with. It is the primary battle for the soul in a domain where knowledge (or at least data) are abundant and at the fingertips- but the capacity to keep the attention and analyze data to make meaning has atrophied. The last decade has witnessed the emergence and dissolution of national, political, and cyber borders- with the addition of oxymorons such as "fake news" and "trolls" in the familiar lexicon. With the potentially timely dismantling of hierarchical systems of "news" and expansive utilization of citizen journalism, the line between truth and falsehood has become blurred. "We take the faceless at face value now" (Jackson, 2009). In such a moment, the call to soulful aging claims further attention. The call is not to become a distributor of data but a decipherer of it- to synthesize, metabolize and discern.

> "In the second half of life, we are called to become wise rather than clever, to become authentic rather than manipulative, to become compassionate rather than self-centered." – (Hollis, 2009)

Paradigms for engaging with soulful aging

Decolonizing aging- time is not to be conquered!

While living in colonial neo-liberal capitalistic cis-hetero-patriarchal temporalities, an overwhelming tragedy is experiencing time as an "enslaver." The traditional corporate exchange of time with money has been incorporated into the lives of society's subjects from the beginning. In fact, death is framed as the "end of time," an evil villain in our lives who will undoubtedly win. Much of gerontology and medicine's efforts have been focused towards extending human life and decreasing suffering- positioning disease and frailty, which inherently come with aging, as the enemy. The wear and tear which comes with aging is seen as an imperfection rather than indices of growth and maturation. However, even this understanding of imperfection can be improved with greater reverence for uniqueness. The Japanese art of Kintsugi, involving the repair of broken pottery with lacquer mixed with rare metals (gold, silver or platinum) highlights the crack in the pottery rather than muting it. It emphasizes the idea of "wabi-sabi" which is about embracing imperfection and the unique traits of individual pieces rather than shuttling towards mass production of "perfect" pieces. It is the crack (or the wrinkle, bruise, broken heart etc.) which as Leonard Cohen and Rumi said let the light (compassion, wisdom) in rather than a flawless veneer. Aging is a big business within a capitalistic medical model- yet- the soul refuses to be monetized or commodified.

> *She asked me the hardest of question- one which has no right to go away! She told me to make a choice about my gender transition- to go through it or not – by actually thinking about it and not, not answering it by default. I owe myself that much dignity, she said. The question has forced me to address questions of what is truly important (embodiment) over what feels important (safety).*

[describing and reflecting on the impacts of a conversation with a mentor in my journal]
Gillani 12/1/2000

It must be acknowledged that even though global citizens are impacted by colonialism, its impacts of indigenous populations are severe and long-lasting. According to the United Nations (United Nations, n.d, p. 2), "Indigenous communities, peoples and nations are those which, having a historical continuity with pre-invasion and pre-colonial societies that developed on their territories, consider themselves distinct from other sectors of the societies now prevailing on those territories. They hold at present non-dominant sectors of society and are determined to preserve, develop and transmit to future generations their ancestral territories and their ethnic identity, as the basis of their continued existence as peoples, in accordance with their own cultural patterns, social institutions and legal system." The Declaration on the Rights of Indigenous Peoples (UN, n.d) recognizes that indigenous peoples have "suffered from historic injustices as a result of their colonization" (p. 2).

Colonization was not a one and done event. The West continues to colonize Indigenous communities and communities of color- though it's vehicles of control and conquest may have changed appearance. Colonization was and is a severely traumatic experience, as it is a sudden, shocking, comprehensive mode of domination imposed from outside (Bogdan, 2014). Subjugation was brutal and enforced through military force, genocide, epistimicide, imprisonment, boarding schools, and euro-centric laws (Bogdan, 2014).

A significant impact of colonialism is the decimation of indigenous ways of thinking about time, aging, and, consequently, the value of soulful aging. Many indigenous communities treat time more from a descriptive point of view and give at least equal weight to time as an eternal quality". For example within some aboriginal communities from New Zealand (Mauri name "Aotearoa" loosely translates the "land of the long white cloud.") history is a concept that "moves across past, present, and future. (Shipley, 1998)" Much of this eternal quality comes from Mauri Aboriginal cosmology is centered on 'The Dreaming' (Gallois, 2007) - which may be a nod towards the unconscious. Therefore, time does not exist as a horizontal line but rather in a vertical relationship to the present. "The past underlies and is within the present, 'events do not happen now, as a result of a chain of events extending back to . . . a beginning. They exist, and they happen because that Dreamtime is also here and now. It is The Dreaming, the condition or ground of existence.' It is sacred-past-in-the-present" (Roque, 2022).

Therefore, to seriously consider soulful aging, one must step out of the ubiquitous paradigms of colonialist transactional time and engage with time and relationships from a non-transactional perspective. I propose that reparations, whether to indigenous or enslaved communities, commitment to community-based living, and distancing the Self from domination and ownership of others are all salient features of decolonizing aging. Community might be considered a proxy for such a life. Donna Haraway, the revolutionary contemporary academic, expresses this as "I am sick to death of bonding through kinship and "the family," and I long for models of solidarity and human unity and difference rooted in friendship, work, partially shared purposes, intractable collective pain, inescapable mortality, and persistent hope ... Ties through blood ... have been bloody enough already. (Schneider, 2017)"

It is our colonized relationship with aging which has desecrated notions of community and legacy, prompting individuals to funnel all their resources into their blood "family" rather than seeing all humans and more than human creatures as one large family. Accumulation of resources amongst the elite few (many who read this article would be considered part of this group) leads to suffering of all. Decolonizing aging means that we would learn to let go of the desire to leave a legacy on the earth with only our genetic off-springs. We will see, as our ancestors did that, we leave our marks every day we live on this planet and the best possible legacy we can have is a healthier, kinder planet. By decolonizing aging, we will be able to step away from extractivist activities and relationships and develop a deeper solidarity with the flora and fauna around us. When we will have the audacity to feel with and for the planet, we will no longer need to conquer and colonize it. Instead, we will recognize her as our "creator" and find boundless joy in serving her in a symbiotic fashion (Kimmerer, 2022).

As a primarily white settler colonial society, we cannot simply disavow the damage perpetuated or benefits gained by colonialism. Neither can we claim to live decolonized lives or progress in decolonized aging without intentional attention and action in this area. Soulful aging requires stepping away from the dichotomized narratives of traditionalists and activists, learning from those outcasts by society, and building upon communal capital. There is no need to reinvent the wheel. Indigenous scholars and leaders are already leading the way in decolonizing society, and those interested in soulful aging must seek to learn from and pay homage to these leaders (Braun et al., 2013). The stance of challenging the status quo while simultaneously supporting the disenfranchised is mentioned by Donna Haraway when she states, "Our task is to make trouble, to stir up potent response to devastating events, as well as to settle troubled waters and rebuild quiet places. (O'Connell, 2016)". The tasks of questioning existing paradigms while simultaneously holding sacred spaces of silence have been traditionally held and performed by the elders of a community- but within the Anthropocene, with the basic nature of time being questioned- perhaps the task falls upon all those who are soulfully aging? Ultimately the call for soulful aging might require the individual to decolonize time within themSelves.

> *"Decolonizing time" involves the cultivation of the capacity to be still, to listen and not to be self-certain . . . I think means learning to inhabit these times of urgent trouble with a memory that this is not and has never been all of time, including all of now – that we do not live in a time only of domination; we also live in times of tremendous flourishing and generativity and capacities to connect with each other.*- Donna Haraway "On Decolonizing Time".

An important part of decolonizing aging is letting go of our sense of "ownership"- whether that is of ourselves, the land or even the boundaries between what is "me" and what is the "other". After going through a process of spiritual aging from a decolonized perspective, author Richard Powers, author of the book "The Overstory" -when asked if his time with the redwoods changed him answered "It depends on what you mean by you. In the sense that we're most familiar with it now, that that kind of private individual, yeah sure humility and fear and insignificance. But that's not a genuine or legitimate perception of being. It's a cultural illusion. If you allow kinship then the question of you becomes more permeable and what happened to me along the way was I began to identify across species boundaries. I began to feel like the journey is so profoundly imbricated and knotted together that my own destiny was the destiny these other things. we're not anywhere near or separate as I thought we were when I started the journey. So did I become smaller or vulnerable yes but I also became larger. In Whitman-esque way I started to contain multitudes or they started to contain me." (Vaughan-Lee, 2023)

Hence within the concept of soulful aging, decolonizing time refers to the process of challenging and reimagining the dominant ways of understanding and organizing time that colonial powers have imposed. This includes examining and rejecting the Eurocentric models and systems of timekeeping that have been used to oppress and marginalize people. Colonial epistimicide of ancient knowledge distanced the soul from engaging with the present. Extending oneself to kin beyond blood and boundaries, growing within realms of wisdom and self-knowledge, and identifying known and ancient ways of knowing may be some strategies for decolonizing soulful aging. Reclaiming our personal elderhood and recognizing the elders around us with rituals, respect, and resonance may mature the process of soulful aging.

Queering aging

Colonization is the water we swim in. All members of western society are deeply impacted by colonial thought and reap both benefits and confinement from historical colonial practices. However, even within the mire of colonial thinking, many marginalized communities have developed strategies of resistance leading to relatively liberatory practices. The Queer community may be identified as one of these communities.

The term "Queer" has a complex history and has been used in a variety of ways over time. The term 'Queer' was originally used as a derogatory term for LGBTQ+ people, but many LGBTQ+ individuals and communities have reclaimed it as a term of pride and self-identification. The process of reclaiming the word 'Queer' began in the 1980s when it was used as a rallying cry by HIV/AIDS activists, who sought to reclaim the word and use it as a term of pride and empowerment (Hines & Wright, 2017). It has become increasingly common in the past few decades and is often used as a term for self-identity. In this manuscript, Queer includes individuals who do not identify with the LGBTQ+ community but all who do not fit within the normative definitions of youth, beauty, and power. Queering aging practices include queering time, queering silence and solitude, and queering embodiment to enhance soulful aging.

Queering aging is a distinct notion from decolonizing aging. It allows for a multiplicity of pathways, life courses and even relationship structures across an individual's life span. Queering aging in an invitational space for all those committed to a journey of soulfully aging without falling in to the confinement of cis-heteropatriarchal. Apart from shifting one's relationship from ownership and domination to collaboration using decolonizing aging, queering aging allows individuals to consider epistemic multiplicity and identify novel imaginal life patterns.

Queering time

With the term queer being reclaimed, many concepts connected to queerness are also being reclaimed (Adames & Chavez-Dueñas, 2021). This reclamation is helpful for all individuals, whether they identify with the LGBTQ+ community or not. One example of it is the notion of Queer time. Over time, LGBTQ+ individuals have not wanted to and/or not been allowed to exist on the same life course as the general population to varying degrees. However, queer activists and leaders have challenged the perception of being excluded from turning point events such as marriage, having kids, etc., into a notion of empowerment. Hence, now Queer time refers to how LGBTQ+ individuals and communities experience and conceptualize time differently from dominant cultural norms. It challenges traditional notions of linear, heteronormative time and instead embraces a more fluid and non-binary understanding of time- where individuals feel the freedom to pursue happiness and goals at all stages of life." Queer time is characterized by a non-linear, non-teleological and non-normative approach and relationship to time. It provides that time is not bound by traditional notions of progress, development and linearity- rather- it is open ended, non-hierarchical and non-predictable (Halberstam, 2011).

The notion of queer aging can be integrated into the idea of soulful aging. Engagement with queer time allows folx to age at the calling of their soul, resisting dominant norms and expectations rather than retreat to the pre-established routes of existence. It opens new options and possibilities for individuals at different life junctures, liberating them from the confines of patterns established by those before then. Queer time can also provide folx the capacity to pursue unbidden pleasures and desires. By explicitly decolonizing cis-hetero-patriarchal timelines and developing a more flexible and malleable perspective around timelines, individuals can create more space in their lives-to fully live.

> *As we age, time becomes more flexible. The past becomes present and the future becomes now. This fluidity can be disorienting, but it can also be an opportunity to let go of old certainties and embrace new possibilities. (Hollis, 2018)*

Queering silence towards solitude

Another term for reclamation is that of Queer Silence. Traditionally, Queer silence has referred to how LGBTQ+ individuals and communities are often rendered invisible or marginalized within mainstream culture and society. It is a concept that highlights how dominant cultural narratives can exclude or erase the experiences and perspectives of LGBTQ+ people. Another interpretation of Queer silence is how LGBTQ+ people have been forced to silence their identities and loves to gain fickle safety and transactional negative liberty (Carter, 2021) from the society. However, with reclamation, Queer silence can be converted into solitude- a place that can invite individuals to hold space for the "negative" or "emptiness" in their lives. By embodying a "queer" demeanor towards life, one may be able to distance themselves from the world's noise and develop motion towards stillness and, with it, self-knowledge. This was explained by Peabody award winner radio show host Krista Tippets (2021) as "One of the great challenges of life is to learn to be alone peaceably, at home in oneself. The pandemic has forced many of us, at best, to work out the difference between isolation and loneliness or to find "ease within the aloneness inside ourselves" (Batchelor, 2021). Within a capitalistic regime where silence is antithetical to consumerism, quietude is often identified as failure or defeat. It is also synonymized by stagnation and a deterioration of progress. However, all of these are colonized notions of silence. "Silence is not stillness, but movement; and therefore the graveyard of any fixed identity. Real silence puts any present understanding to shame; orphans us from certainty; leads us beyond the well-known and accepted reality and confronts us with the unknown and previously unacceptable conversation about to break in upon our lives (Whyte, 2020)."Within soulful aging, queering silence towards solitude, holding it not as a harsh vow of silence but a gentle "house of belonging" (Whyte, 2021b) initiates a sense of wisdom, compassion, and the ability to envision a third way without a compulsion to solve every riddle. It allows the individual to move from feeling isolated to creating a sense of belonging with the Self.

Another way LGBTQ+ individuals have been "silenced" is through social isolation through discrimination. This can be a particularly acute problem for LGBTQ+ people who live in areas with little support or acceptance of their identity or who may face barriers to accessing social networks and community connections. Research has shown that LGBTQ+ people are at higher risk for poor mental health outcomes, including depression, anxiety, and suicidality, due in part to the social isolation and stigma they may face. However, queer individuals are not the only ones who experience stigmatized isolation from society. Research has shown that older adults who report high levels of social isolation are at higher risk for poor physical health outcomes, including a greater likelihood of developing chronic conditions such as hypertension and diabetes. Elder isolation has also been linked to an increased risk of cognitive decline and dementia. In addition, older adults who experience social isolation may be at greater risk for poor mental health outcomes, including depression, anxiety, and suicidality (JB et al., 2021).

Hence both communities suffer greatly from "silencing" from social isolation and stigmatization. Queer solitude is identified as the shift many LGBTQ + individuals may experience from "loneliness" to "solitude." Queer solitude may be envisioned as a coping strategy but can be seen as a springboard for social, emotional, and spiritual well-being. Queer solitude brings within it a deep sense of self. May Sarton distinguishes between loneliness and solitude by saying "Loneliness is the poverty of self; solitude is richness of self." By shifting the frame of understanding from isolation to solitude, the soulful aging may find deeper belonging within themselves, self-sufficiency within their often-limited community, and enhance their sense of wholeness. This concept is explained by Henri Nouwen, who held exemplified queer solitude and soulful aging through his service and spirituality.

> To live a spiritual life, we must first find the courage to enter into the desert of our loneliness and to change it by gentle and persistent efforts into a garden of solitude. The movement from loneliness to solitude, however, is the beginning of any spiritual life because it is the movement from the restless senses to the restful spirit, from the outward-reaching cravings to the inward-reaching search, from the fearful clinging to the fearless play. (Nouwen, 2004)

It can be argued that many of the world's spiritual leaders engaged in what may be referred to as Queer solitude. They were shunned by society and withdrew from it on their own accord- providing their soul the time and space to hear it's true calling and go through it's mission. Whether we think of Jesus of Nazareth's forty day battle with temptation during his hike in the wilderness, Prophet Mohammed receiving revelations after a 30 day meditation stretch in the Cave of Illuminations, or Rumi providing the planet with over five thousand poems after leaving his home town and society, all these spiritual gurus chose to give their souls plenty of solitude- respite from the noise in their society to truly connect with the Divine.

Queering embodiment

An essential feature of soulful aging is a deep embodiment of the individual and a non-self-indulgent relationship with pleasure. I propose that looking at aging and embodiment from a queer perspective will consider individuals of all ages not just as bodies with sexual needs but also as erotic beings with diverse sexualities to be celebrated and desired In a society where many aging folks are considered sexless and genderless creatures, soulful aging embodiment becomes a unique reflection of queer embodiment. (Silver, 2003) By removing shame from sexuality and supporting individuals in affirming their inherent beauty and worth at all ages, Queering embodied aging would enable people to step away from stigmatized beliefs about the Self and others. Queering embodied aging implies not the denial of aging nor the pedestalization of youth or age, but rather it would be an embracing and appreciating of both abilities and disabilities (Fabbre, 2017). Additionally, it includes openness to the changing human experience with age, its integration with erotic freedom in all ages, and the changes this brings to human relationships.

Befriending aging- time to bid farewell

> Old age can be a time of clearance. In old age, as your life calms, you will be able to make many clearances in order to see who you are, what life has done to you, and what you have made of your life . . . False burdens can fall away in old age. (O'donohue, 2005)

A large part of soulful aging is giving up the archetypal dream of immortality and recognizing the human body's limitations. Capitalism and the medical model, overlapping with an existential individual level desire for immortality and potential fear of death, push individuals to fear death and extend life regardless of its quality or impact on others. Soulful aging offers a counter narrative to running away from aging and invites a befriending of the Self within it.

> Aging is not just decay; it's growth. It is about growing in wisdom, learning to live more fully, and deepening our connection with Self and others. It's the continuation of the journey you have been on all your life. The journey has a destination, and that is where I am going. (Palmer, 2000)

Hence, growth, change, and, ultimately, bodily death are inherent parts of the journey. There is no choice in this matter. Soulful aging calls for a humble posture with which one interacts with death, whether it is with argument, fear, or curiosity (Oliver, 2000), and how one ultimately deals with their reactions to death.

> Death, I think, is a passage, not a place to stay. It's a right of way, a passage. It's the way love passes on. (Tippetts, 2020)

Imbibed with all forms of love (eros, agape, philia), soulful aging invites a sense of befriending death within society. It challenges perceptions of time and eternity and, with it evokes movement away from transactional relationships to one of mutual belonging and understanding. Without befriending death, one is constantly in existential fear.

> *Befriending death seems to be the basis of all other forms of befriending. I have a deep sense, hard to articulate, that if we could really befriend death we would be free people. So many of our doubts and hesitations, ambivalences and insecurities are bound up with our deep-seated fear of death that our lives would be significantly different if we could relate to death as a familiar guest instead of a threatening stranger* (O'rourke, 2010).

All beginnings end- and endings begin

> *"When do I fully claim my masculinity? Is it when I "pass" or when I feel fully embodied within my forever changing body. Similarly, when do I claim being a grown up? Is it when the legal system claims I am adult, I develop dependents (and dependencies) or is it when I "feel" grown up. Does one ever fully embody an identity or are we all constantly growing- in flux- as multitudes" [written as my new year reflection while grappling with my emerging identities 12/31/2022] Gillani, 2022*

I bring forth the humble conclusion that soulful aging is a process in itself. It includes moments of deep ecstasy and dark nights of the soul, recognition of our Divinity and complete humility (from the word humus, belonging to the earth), and recognition of time being finite and yet holding eternity as a valid possibility (Mary Oliver, When death comes). The tools for soulful aging are then as paradoxical as the process itself. This manuscript identifies some constructs which might be useful for soulful aging, but there is no doubt that many of them still remain unexamined and undeclared. Ultimately, blessings from the sages and universe might be required to support all of us who are involved in the harrowing, exciting, and terrifying journey of soulful aging. Soulful aging is an inside job- but one which may be supported by engaging with some of the paradigms mentioned above.

Acknowledgments

As mentioned above, this manuscript could not have been developed without decades of toil and labor from my mentors. Soulful aging demands deviance from traditional academic norms of claiming any of the above material as strictly mine (though I acknowledge that I have written it myself!). The ideas, concepts and the skill to weave them into a coherent narrative were all generously poured in me with my multitudes of mentors. These include authors (printed and not), poets, prophets, academics and sages of all variety. I want to especially acknowledge Drs. Andy Achenbaum, Peter Hovmand, Vanessa Fabbre and KJ Cerankowski for their unconditional positive regard and unwavering trust in my becoming me. I am honored to be standing on the shoulder of giants. Anything good in this manuscript is attributed to them. All errors are mine.

Disclosure statement

No potential conflict of interest was reported by the author.

ORCID

Braveheart Gillani http://orcid.org/0000-0002-4637-3983

References

Adames, H. Y., & Chavez-Dueñas, N. Y. (2021). Reclaiming all of me: The racial queer identity framework. In K. L. Nadal & M. R. Scharrón-Del Río (Eds.), *Queer Psychology*. Springer. https://doi.org/10.1007/978-3-030-74146-4_4

Albinsson, P. A., & Yasanthi Perera, B. (2012). Alternative marketplaces in the 21st century: Building community through sharing events. *Journal of Consumer Behavior, 11*(4), 303–315. https://doi.org/10.1002/cb.1389

Batchelor, S. (2021, September 24). *Finding ease in aloneness*. The on Being Project. Retrieved March 10, 2023, from https://onbeing.org/programs/stephen-batchelor-finding-ease-in-aloneness/

Bauckham, R., & Hart, T. (n.d). The shape of time. *The Future as God's Gift: Explorations in Christian Eschatology*. https://doi.org/10.5040/9780567660503.ch-003

Bianchi, E. C. (2011). *Aging as a spiritual journey*. Wipf & Stock Publishers.

Bogdan, Ş. (2014). Late (for) modernity: Transition and the traumatic colonization of the future of post communist cultures. *Literature and the Long Modernity*, 355–367. https://doi.org/10.1163/9789401210959_025

Borges, J. L., Yates, D., Irby, J. E., Feinstein, A., André, M., & Packer, N. (2007). *Labyrinths: selected stories and other writings*. The Folio Society.

Boschung, D. (2013). Prospects. *Kairos as a Figuration of Time*, 53–54. https://doi.org/10.30965/9783846756140_006

Braun, K. L., Browne, C. V., Ka'opua, L. S., Kim, B. J., & Mokuau, N. (2013). Research on indigenous elders: From positivistic to decolonizing methodologies. *The Gerontologist, 54*(1), 117–126. https://doi.org/10.1093/geront/gnt067

Campbell, J. (2020). *The hero with a thousand faces*. Joseph Campbell Foundation.

Carter, I. (2021, November 19). *Positive and negative liberty*. Stanford Encyclopedia of Philosophy. Retrieved January 26, 2023, from https://plato.stanford.edu/entries/liberty-positive-negative/

Clare, E. (2017). *Brilliant imperfection grappling with cure*. Duke University Press.

Emlet, C. A. (2016). Stigma in an aging context. *Interdisciplinary Topics in Gerontology and Geriatrics*, 144–158. https://doi.org/10.1159/000448560

Fabbre, V. (2017). Queer aging: Implications for social work practice with lesbian, gay, bisexual, transgender, and queer older adults. *Social Work, 62*(1), 73–76.

Gallois, W. (2007). *Time, religion and history*. Longman.

Gibran, K. (2008). *On time. In the prophet: By Kahlil Gibran. essay*. Alfred A. Knopf.

Halberstam, J. (2011). *The queer art of failure*. Duke University Press.

Hines, S., & Wright, J. (2017). Queer temporality and ageing: Interrupting normative linear time. *Ageing & Society, 37*(1), 1–20.

Hollis, J. (2006). Chapter five. (essay.). In *Finding meaning in the second half of life - how to finally really grow up* (p. 98). Gotham Books.

Hollis, J. (2010). *What matters most: Living a more considered life*. Gotham Books.

Hollis, J. (2018). *Living an examined life: Wisdom for the second half of the journey*. Sounds True.

Hope, S. (2005). Embodied knowledge and disembodied ignorance: A reflection on the 'ways of knowing' conference. *Anthropology in Action, 12*(2). *Anthropology in Action, 12*(2). https://doi.org/10.3167/096720105793233995

Jackson, M. (2009). *Distracted: The erosion of attention and the coming dark age*. Prometheus Books.

Jalāl Al-Dīn, R., & Barks, C. (2003). *Rumi: The book of love: Poems of ecstasy and longing*. HarperOne, HarperCollins.

Jb, H-L, J., & S T, B. L. (n.d.). *Social relationships and mortality risk: A meta-analytic review.* PLoS medicine. Retrieved January 26, 2023, from https://pubmed.ncbi.nlm.nih.gov/20668659/

Kadri, A., Gracey, F., & Leddy, A. (2022). What factors are associated with posttraumatic growth in older adults? A systematic review. *Clinical Gerontologist*, 1–18. https://doi.org/10.1080/07317115.2022.2034200

Kalanithi, P. (2020). Prologue: The beginning of the end. (essay.). In *When breath becomes air* (p. 9). Vintage Classics.

Kimmerer, R. W. (2022). *Braiding Sweetgrass.* Langara College.

Kinship with the more than human world. To The Best of Our Knowledge. (2022, March 15). Retrieved January 25, 2023 from https://www.ttbook.org/series/kinship

Krista, T. (2021, September 24). *Stephen Batchelor - finding ease in aloneness.* The On Being Project. Retrieved January 26, 2023, from https://onbeing.org/programs/stephen-batchelor-finding-ease-in-aloneness/

Lindsay, J., M, M., Anderson, T. J., & Saunders, N. (2021, April 5). *Folx.* New Discourses. Retrieved January 26, 2023, from https://newdiscourses.com/tftw-folx/

Macfarlane, R. (2020). *Under land a deep time journey.* Penguin Books.

Newport, C. (2019). *Deep work.* Walker-Summary?.

Nouwen, H. J. M. (2004). *Out of solitude: Three meditations on the Christian life.* Ave Maria Press.

O'Connell, M. (2016, November 20). *Staying-with the trouble: Haraway and the cthulhucene.* Posthuman Aesthetics. Retrieved March 10, 2023, from https://open-tdm.au.dk/ph/2016/11/staying-with-the-trouble-haraway-and-the-cthulhucene/#:~:text=Our%20task%20is%20to%20make,some%20mythical%20past%20is%20worst.

O'donohue, J. (1998). *Annam Cara.* Lindhardt og Ringhof.

O'donohue, J. (2005). *Beauty: The invisible embrace.* Perennial.

Oliver, M. (2000). *When Death Comes. In the leaf and the cloud: A poem. essay.* Da Capo press.

Oliver, M. (2020). The Journey. In *Devotions: The selected poems of Mary Oliver. essay.* Penguin Group USA.

O'rourke, M. (2010). *Befriending death: Henri Nouwen and a spirituality of dying.* Orbis Books.

O'tuama, P. (2021, November 8). *Padraig Ó Tuama and Marilyn Nelson – "so let us pick up the stones over which we stumble, friends, and build altars".* The On Being Project. Retrieved January 25, 2023, from https://onbeing.org/programs/padraig-o-tuama-and-marilyn-nelson-so-let-us-pick-up-the-stones-over-which-we-stumble-friends-and-build-altars/

Palmer, P. J. (2000). *Let your life speak: Listening for the voice of vocation.* Jossey-Bass.

Parker, J. C. (2022). Head transplantation and immortality: When is life worth living forever? *The Journal of Medicine and Philosophy: A Forum for Bioethics and Philosophy of Medicine, 47*(2), 279–292. https://doi.org/10.1093/jmp/jhab044

Peck, M. S. (2008). *The road less traveled: A new psychology of love, traditional values and spiritual growth.* Rider.

Roque, C. S. (2022). Chapter 6 on Tjukurrpa, painting up, and building thought. *Explorations in Psychoanalytic Ethnography*, 148–172. https://doi.org/10.1515/9780857456946-008

Schneider, J. (2017). Scientific criticism and the sociology of knowledge. *Professing Sociology*, 17–29. https://doi.org/10.4324/9781315127484-3

Shipley, J. (1998). *Prime Minister's Statement.* Wellington, New Zealand Government.

Silver, C. B. (2003). Gendered identities in old age: Toward (de)gendering? *Journal of Aging Studies*, *17*(4), 379–397. https://doi.org/10.1016/s0890-40650300059-8

Simmons, H. C., & Wilson, J. (2001). *Soulful aging: Ministry through the stages of adulthood.* Smyth & Helwys Pub.

Smart, C. M. (2021). Wisdom mind: Conceptual foundations and preparing to deliver the program. *Wisdom Mind*, 1–18. https://doi.org/10.1093/med-psych/9780197510001.003.0001

Tippets, K. (2020, December 9). '*When things fall apart.*' The on Being Project. Retrieved March 10, 2023, from https://onbeing.org/programs/devendra-banhart-when-things-fall-apart/

United Nations. (n.d.). *The United Nations and decolonization* |. Retrieved January 26, 2023, from https://www.un.org/dppa/decolonization/en

United Nations. (n.d). *United Nations declaration on the rights of indigenous peoples for indigenous peoples*. United Nations. Retrieved March 10, 2023, from https://www.un.org/development/desa/indigenouspeoples/declaration-on-the-rights-of-indigenous-peoples.html

Vaughan Lee, E., McConnell, T., Holten, F. G. K., Steinauer-Scudder, C., & Vaughan Lee, A. L. E. (2023, January 31). Kinship, community, and consciousness – with Richard Powers. *Emergence Magazine*. Retrieved January 31, 2023 from https://emergencemagazine.org/interview/kinship-community-and-consciousness/

Walcott, D. (2011). *White egrets: Poems*. Farrar, Straus and Giroux.

Whyte, D. (1999). *Fire in the earth poems*. Many Rivers Press.

Whyte, D. (2011a, June 15). *10 questions that have no right to go away*. Oprah.com. Retrieved January 26, 2023, from https://www.oprah.com/oprahs-lifeclass/poet-david-whytes-questions-that-have-no-right-to-go-away_1/all#:~:text=Questions%20that%20have%20no%20right%20to%20go%20away%20are%20those,or%20without%20our%20conscious%20participation.

Whyte, D. (2011b). *The house of belonging: Poems*. Many Rivers Press.

Whyte, D. (2019). *The bell and the blackbird*. Many Rivers Press.

Whyte, D. (2023). *Solitude. In consolations: The solace, nourishment and underlying meaning of everyday words*. essay, Canongate Books.

"Take my hand, precious lord and lead me home": witnessing soulful aging

Karen Skerrett

ABSTRACT

This essay reflects the author's personal and professional dedication to understanding how some individuals create life affirming, growth filled stories while others, also faced with challenges fail to flourish. Weaving together current thinking on adult development, the growth of the storied self, the cultivation of resilience in couples and families and ongoing research with older adults, the author infuses her clinical experiences as a psychologist with findings from a variety of research projects highlighting the many ways people traverse the aging process and reevaluate their place in the world. Integrating a personal dimension throughout. The author narrates her own exploration of soulful aging and the response to an inner call to repair and renew.

My mother read the Bible

This is an ordinary, almost unremarkable memory for some. For me, such a memory is surprising and foreign. I recently woke in the middle of the night and clearly saw the soft leather book, its edges frayed and pages yellowed, held in my mother's two hands. It was an astonishing image, not just in its clarity but in its arrival in my consciousness at all. I had locked up shop on my memories of my mother since her sudden death just months after my twelfth birthday. As an only child, adopted at birth, my world revolved around her. In the space of a few days, that world was dismantled and my stability and security upended; the adored North Star of my life was lost forever.

For years after, I dreamed that I would come home from school and find her in her familiar spot at the kitchen stove; she would greet me with a warm smile and welcoming hug, as if it were I who had been away. I learned early that grief comes in waves, swelling and gathering force against the rocks, breaking when we least expect it.

My father, who slipped into his own depression following her death, faced the daunting task of raising a soon-to-be adolescent daughter. Up to that time, I had seen him as a distant, stern, serious man with high expectations for my behavior. Somewhere in the deeper recesses of my mind, I made a pivotal decision: I would intensify my efforts to be the best, most self-sufficient, need-free daughter he could ask for. If I could earn my keep, and not require much from him but rather make life easier for him, the chances of a secure future would be higher. These thoughts solidified the framework for my earliest storyline: *Please keep me. I'll show you how good I am, and I'll make you glad you didn't send me away.* My success at this effort also paid off a debt I felt I owed my parents for taking me in, for adopting me in the first place.

For most of my life, people have described me as someone with "soul." I might have felt more flattered if I had had a clue what that meant. I remember deriving meaning from synchronicities or interesting occurrences, such as the one in which my favorite music box, a gift from my mother, stopped working the morning of her death. Having been raised by devout Swedish Lutheran parents with weekly church and Sunday School habits, I had heard the words *soul* and *spirit* from the pulpit, but as I got older, I didn't think it particularly fashionable to be vocal about my spiritual interests.

An introvert by temperament and nurtured by growing up in solitude, I was drawn to English literature in high school, philosophy and religion in college. I believed that it was essentially up to me to make sense of life, so I developed a reflective habit that is now like a second skin.

Over the past five years or so, I have begun to notice that I could recall the name of my high school music teacher more readily than what I had eaten for breakfast or the names of characters on the show I was currently streaming. I wondered, is this my *entre* to elderhood? Despite arthritic knees and hips, I am quite physically active, grateful for my high energy level. Ever the problem solver, I figured perhaps more word games or crosswords would be the solution to my lack of recall.

The image of my mother's hands that night felt like something else entirely: organic, mysterious, powerful. I have come to call these experiences a visitation from the soul, or (in a riff on what my Catholic friends would call a "near occasion of sin") a "near occasion of soul." Arising unbidden, drenched with meaning, they are not a moment in time but rather a simulacrum of imagery, preblended by time and memory, feelings and thoughts, intermingled like a rich stew. I knew a fair amount about aging, both theoretical and personal, but prior to the invitation to write this essay, I had only an intellectual notion of "soulful aging." I decided that considering them separately might be the path to greater clarity. Before landing on my own definition of *soul*, I went in search of more experiential evidence: where had these experiences occurred before, and was there anything I could do to elicit them?

A definition takes shape

One of my first experiences was when I was sitting on the shore of Lake Michigan, feeling as one with the waves, transfixed by their rhythmic beauty. Nature has long been my sacred space, the one place in which my gratitude is immediate and gripping. I suddenly recalled a moment when I was watching my granddaughter in a dance class. She was apart from the other girls, moving her little four-year-old body to "Somewhere Over the Rainbow." As I watched, I wondered, was I ever that unselfconscious, ever that in tune with my body to express its authentic rhythms? Tears began to run down my face. I felt I couldn't contain my overwhelming love for my young granddaughter. It was a tender, heart-touching moment, certainly, but so much more. Named after my birth mother, my granddaughter's dancing led me backward and forward across four generations of women, linked by an essence that felt timeless. I realize now this was a soul connection.

Music has always struck me as a doorway to the soul; I never fail to weep when I listen to Morten Lauridsen's "Magnum Mysterium," the haunting composition that describes the wonderment of the animals as they gaze on Christ in the manger. Then, too, I think of the gospel services I have attended in my native Chicago. It is no wonder that the African American culture is synonymous with the word *soul*: soul food, soul brothers and sisters, soul music, soul train. A gritty vocal style expresses music that is all about naked emotion, personal testimony, and a complex amalgam of the atrocities of slavery and the resilience of the human spirit. It is hope born in struggle; it is "singing with the ugly face," as gospel singer Sharon Jones describes. The recent Disney Pixar film *Soul* is both a celebration of African American culture and a reflection on the meaning of existence.

As in other areas of life, perhaps the best definition of soul is the simplest. I've come to believe that soul is our essence, the aspect of a human being that connects us to the universal, spiritual nature of everything. Every religious and spiritual tradition teaches that one's deeper identity (e.g., Buddha nature, Christ nature, Atman) rests on shedding egoic preoccupations (Rohr, 2011; Rohr, 2013; Zweig, 2021). Our sense of self can be rooted in ego or rooted in soul. Whether we are walking in the woods, listening to music, or making soup, it is not about what we're doing but how the doing brings us closer to a soulful expression, and that takes time, presence, and above all, attention.

John O'Donohue calls the soul our "textured presence." He writes, "What you separate the soul joins. As your experience extends and deepens, your memory becomes richer and more complex. Your soul is the priestess of memory, selecting, sifting, and ultimately gathering your vanishing days towards presence" (O'Donohue, 1997, p. 118).

When I speak to clients or watch my adult children (now in their early forties), I'm reminded of myself at their age: juggling multiple roles, running breathlessly from one thing to the next, reprioritizing multiple needs, and trying to excel on the professional, home, and community fronts all at once. The only conversation I had with a higher power then was to bargain for more hours in a day. Fortunately, as I began to move through my fifties, I experienced a beginning awareness of my subjective sense of time.

Identified by one of my teachers, Bernice Neugarten, subjective sense of time is the idea that we carry within us a sense of what is a "normal" time to accomplish various tasks or stages of the life cycle (Neugarten, 1972). This sense of timeliness – the best time to marry, to become a parent, to retire – are all socially constructed and further shaped by the particular cohort and family experiences we are brought up in. This is the dimension that most shapes our stories and results in our effort to draw a continuous thread through our discontinuous lives. Passing the midpoint of life, which signals that we have less time ahead than time since birth, alters our perspective and may stimulate a reorientation. This transition definitely presents opportunities for change and growth, yet whether this shift in orientation arrives as a tug on the sleeve or a punch on the arm, moving into fuller awareness is more difficult for some than others. I have often longed for a life cycle shaman, someone to escort me through time, to point the way, to alert me to pitfalls on the path and opportunities for love. Reflecting on my earliest storyline and its do-it-myself theme, I realize that I have shaped a career that enabled me to be that person for others and, ultimately, as a way to give to myself.

For more than forty years, I have had a privileged position as story catcher for the lives of clients, students, and research participants, first as a nurse, then as a clinical psychologist. I have regularly sat with people as they struggled with a panorama of life challenges. At some point, almost every one of them asks a version of the question, "What does this mean, and what do I do about it?" The issue of how to find meaning and craft a life that reflects that meaning have long driven both my personal and professional lives. Indelibly shaped by my mentor Mihalyi Csikszentmihalyi, who identified the concept of "flow" and the ingredients of an optimal life (Csikszentmihalyi & Csikszentmihalyi, 1988), I continue to be a passionate student of human development, hooked on the study and exploration of the life story. My experiences as a story catcher are my best and favorite teachers, adding rich fertilizer to the compost of my own seedlings of soul.

A longer story than ever before

How, then, to understand soulful aging? Aging is often described as moving into the twilight of life. I was ambivalent about that metaphor until I realized that light is at its most magical at twilight; latent colors that were overpowered by sun or shaded by clouds during the day become free to emerge with greater depth and beauty.

Never before in human history have adults had so many years of life. Baby boomers – people born between 1946 and 1964—have added to the population surge of adults over sixty-five, now projected to rise to 400 million by 2050 (Mather et al., 2015). In applying the metaphor for our lives as a book with three acts – a beginning, middle, and end – each act now contains many more scenes. Tens of millions of us will make it to act 3. This third act is far from a redo of the first or second. It is, in life, what it is in a book: the time of a story's climax, denouement, and resolution. It can also be a time of transformation (Skerrett, 2022).

Our culture continues to have a wildly ambivalent relationship to aging, vacillating between stories of decline and reinvention, and typically homogenizes people at either end of the continuum. Even the most recent projections of the life course insufficiently anticipated the complexity of a longer life span. I regularly take every chance I get to encourage my students, clients, and anyone else who will listen to examine their own stereotypes of aging, as I find ageism to be a particularly stubborn prejudice (Gullette, 2004). The work of Becca Levy, an epidemiologist at Yale, has made great strides in busting these myths, exposing how negative societal messages about aging impact our health and well-being (Levy, 2022). Even professionals vastly overestimate the problems of later life and underestimate the resilience (Hinrichsen, 2023).

For most of us, early, middle, late, and advanced stages of adulthood are significantly different from each other. The changes are imperceptible initially, then continue to spiral until they become too obvious to ignore. The longevity factor and the individual diversity of the aging process have brought scholars of the life span back to the drawing board for more slicing and dicing of time. The years between sixty-five and eighty are now referred to as the "third age" or the "young-old," and the years from eighty and on as the "fourth age" or the "old-old." There is even a burgeoning scholarship on centenarians, those aged one hundred and older (Diehl et al., 2020). The dividing line between the third and fourth ages may be the murkiest, and the healthiest among us probably don't see ourselves as crossing that line until our late seventies.

For more than twenty-five years, I have been involved in a variety of studies examining life cycle development and resilience (Skerrett & Fergus, 2015; Skerrett et al., 2021; Skerrett, 2016, 2022). Together with observations from decades of clinical practice with adults, I have sought to understand how it is that some individuals create life-affirming, growth-filled stories, while others, also faced with challenges, fail to flourish. Applying a story arc, with a beginning, middle, and end, inclusive of challenges along the way, offers opportunities to identify continuities and discontinuities across time. McAdams (2015) and colleagues advanced this perspective by integrating personality development across the life course with the growth of the storied self (McAdams & Cox, 2010). McAdams (1995) argues that personality follows the internalized and evolving story of the self that one constructs to provide his or her life with unity, purpose, and meaning (McAdams & McLean, 2013).

The Story Project, described elsewhere (Singer & Skerrett, 2014; Skerrett & Fergus, 2015; Skerrett, 2016), studied adults between the ages of twenty-nine and eighty-seven. Volunteers were interviewed in person or responded to questions online, in which they told stories about significant events, memories, challenges, and successes at various points across their life cycle. These stories were then read and evaluated for themes, similarities, and differences across multiple ages and genders. Fifteen years ago, couple stories were added (The Couple Story Project) to further explore the particular components of committed relationships that most contributed to resilient growth and change. My colleague Singer and Skerrett (2014) and I have evaluated the stories of couples together for ten to sixty-four years.

My own experience and those of my clients and research participants carry particular poignancy in these final chapters of life. I like gerontologist Aronson's description of a person's arrival at older adulthood as less a switch thrown than a series of ill-defined thresholds crossed (Aronson, 2019). The years beyond age sixty-five represent greater individual diversity than at any other time in history and at any other point in the life cycle (Arnett et al., 2020). Chronological age becomes at once defining and immaterial. As we live longer and spend many more years in "older age," it is essential to examine the stories we tell about this time and to shape them in ways that better reflect our current realities.

Development between the ages of fifty-five and seventy-five appears to be particularly impacted by complexity, uncertainty, and unanticipated circumstances such as significant illness or the untimely loss of a job, loved family member, or friend. I find that problems emerge when individuals struggle to envision themselves in the alternative roles needed to accommodate these changes. Identities formed around family and work are shaken by prospects of a future that may focus on challenges, health concerns, and potential losses. Development in this period appears to be highly dynamic, simultaneously a time of loss and deterioration and growth and renewal.

Inspired by the work of psychologist Arnett, who proposed the stage of "emerging adulthood," colleagues and I recently proposed a new category called "emerging elderhood" (Arnett, 2015; Skerrett et al., 2021). In an effort to bring greater clarity, and at the risk of adding more murk, we defined the period as one of disequilibrium in roles and identity, an age of feeling in between the structures created by a trajectory of family life, work, and personal milestones.

We observed that the dividing line between older adult and elder varied not only by person but also in the eyes of beholders. It was common to hear someone remark that they felt younger than others saw them, and conversely, if they were challenged by illness, they felt older than they were on paper. We found that the clearest distinction between the two perceptions of aging lies primarily in the health, activities, and social roles of the individual.

There are many complex issues that affect people progressing through the phases of older adulthood, but many have to do with this diversity of the population. Many adults of the same age struggle with the transition between roles that molded their identities, and the reality of those roles having been replaced by retirement, death, and loss. (Skerrett et al., 2021). One sixty-five-year-old is launching children to college, while another is caring for teenage grandchildren. Some sixty-five-year-olds are retiring, while others of the same age are crafting new careers. A seventy-year-old is in a caregiving role for a spouse diagnosed with dementia, while another is moving to a foreign country to set up a new life, .

Clearly, experiences are tied more closely to the psychological and social dimensions than they are to a chronological aging process. With advancing years, health plays a more pivotal role in determining future well-being. Comparing ourselves to others, which we commonly do when we're younger, is pointless at this time, given the wide diversity of this period. This diversity is often exactly what promotes some of my clients to express feeling "rudderless," lacking direction, and unsure of the best course of action.

All of the stories we collected highlighted the complex shifts in adjustment individuals make to facilitate a continued sense of a coherent self. The emergent elders appeared to express a pause in their life story. People with an illusion of having had a singular purpose and identity for most of their adult lives felt lost, purposeless, devalued, and unrecognized when that identity shifted or ended. They grappled with themes around purpose, invisibility, value, direction, and the anticipation of health concerns and disability. However, there were also themes of novelty and opportunity. Adaptation depended on specific personal and social circumstances and the resources individuals were able to mobilize. Development occurred through the exercise of individual agency, in which choices were made amid the opportunities and constraints that recurred across the entire span of life (Elder et al., 2003).

Aging, and this period of transition in particular, invites us to take the long view, tolerate ambiguity, deepen our emotional life, and let go. Without our familiar everyday activities, meanings, and purpose, we can feel unmoored and challenged to craft a story of either decline or growth. Pauses like this transition provide a chance for reflection and reevaluation. While this can happen at any time in life, the pause of emerging elderhood holds greater meaning because it may set the course for all that comes next.

The bulk of my work with later-life adults (and their partners) supports Erikson's formulation that the key task of this phase of the life cycle is to develop integrity, the acceptance of one's life as having been worthwhile (Erikson, 1968). This requires honesty and an alignment of one's values, moral principles, and actions. It involves reconciling past accomplishments with future possibilities, and renouncing regrets. It requires being able to reflect and reminisce about our mistaken expectations, misguided decisions, and missed chances – our "lost possible selves"—and to somehow find the silver linings that benefit our personal complexity and maturity. We need to surrender the rewards associated with early goals and reevaluate our place in the world (Skerrett, 2022). I have been touched by the number of older adults who have told me that truly surrendering those ties to former goals and dreams brings them a surprising feeling of freedom. It is as if they are able to look at those imagined possible selves, now forsaken, with understanding and compassion. Such a lofty task takes time, willingness, and the energy to continue to be curious and engaged with life. It involves acknowledging and accepting the realities of aging; a willingness to accommodate physical, cognitive, and social changes; and an openness to expanding our capacity to tolerate ambiguity and the complexities of our life circumstances.

I have found all of these themes in the stories of older adults. Gerontologist Gene Cohen writes that the drive to tell our life stories in later life is related to an enhanced ability to use both left and right hemispheres (Cohen, 2005). Dan Siegel, founder of relational neurobiology (Siegel, 2016), calls such integration the epitome of mental health. The expanse and variety of neural linkages don't destroy differentiation but rather enhance it. Think of the difference as that between a fruit salad and a smoothie. Our brains are also better at selectivity – the ability to focus on what is important and let the rest go – perhaps a handy byproduct of not being able to remember everything.

As gerontologists Randall and Kenyon suggest, the brain changes associated with aging, along with the luxury of more time and more memories, combine with the inner push to finish our stories (Randall & Kenyon, 2001). These are the perfect conditions to make soulful aging possible.

One seventy-year-old widow put it this way:

> I really never expected that I'd have to be more flexible at this point in my life. I feel like there are so many things to deal with from one day to the next. I expected losing friends or family, but I didn't think I'd have such a hard time getting around or finding new things I can physically do. It seems like there's a lot of uncertainty in my life now. I never thought about having to let people down as much as I do now because I love helping my friends. I'm embarrassed about how much I forget, but I know it could be a lot worse. I've never done so much reminiscing and reflecting, but it seems to help me make sense of it all.

As she well said, older adults are tasked with the prospect of adding new meaning to their life stories by facing regrets; making sense of options; and sorting through new feelings, relationships, and pursuits. We know that a willingness to redefine our sense of purpose benefits both our mental and physical health and acts as a buffer to a variety of life stresses (Skerrett & Fergus, 2015; Skerrett, 2022).

We have good news on the emotional front as well. Throughout adulthood and into old age, our personalities change in positive and adaptive ways. Studies that follow adults over time show that aging brings more positive overall emotional well-being, greater emotional stability, and greater emotional complexity, often referred to as the "positivity bias" (Carstensen et al., 2011). Daily life is reported to be less stressful, and the events that cause stress are experienced as less threatening. Experiencing more positive emotions on a daily basis also increases our longevity by some thirteen years (Marsh et al., 2019).

Such a positive focus extends to our relationships as well, since we get better at being able to see others' perspectives and understanding how they feel. This is linked to an overall increase in marital satisfaction with age (Carstensen et al., 1999). The courageous couples I studied (Skerrett, 2022) bear witness to the transformations that are possible through intentional, ongoing "restorying" along the course of their relationships. They were masters, of a sort, in crafting a team, a "we-focused" relationship. They helped me understand that a positive attitude can operate like a master virtue for relationship development, guiding individual growth and shaping relationship wisdom. It is significant that the components of we-ness that we identified (Singer & Skerrett, 2014) were security, empathy, respect, acceptance, pleasure, humor, and shared meaning and vision (SERAPHS), the "higher angels" of our well-being. It was exciting to notice the similarities between SERAPHS and the ingredients of wisdom, which are management of uncertainty and uncontrollability, optimal levels of resources, reflectivity, and emotional sensitivity and regulation.

Life satisfaction (which peaks around sixty-five) and subjective well-being also increase with age (Staudinger, U., 2020). This complements findings that mental health problems are significantly lower past sixty. By later adulthood, as demands of work and family responsibilities diminish and life is experienced more in the moment, it may be easier to focus on the positive. Clearly, at least until very late in life, aging is not all downhill.

Overall, this time of life sees us shifting to a preventive from a promotional stance toward daily living (Skerrett et al., 2021). In other words, no longer into building up, accumulating, and advancing, older adults winnow their goals to the most important and meaningful – and they are more likely to feel good about it. One eighty-four-year-old put it well: "I just want to hold on to what I've got – my eyesight, my memory, and my husband – as long as I can, but not necessarily in that order!"

As we move into our eighties and beyond, we experience even more ways that the relentless force of gravity brings each of us down to earth. We anticipate death with a myriad of emotions; for some, curiosity and peace; for others, anxiety, resignation, and dread. The specter of widow(er)hood can trigger fears of being alone and, if coupled, the question of who will go first.

The accumulating years may bring more evidence for why Erikson named despair as the alternative to the development of integrity (Erikson, 1968).

Some gerontologists describe the pinnacle or optimal culmination of aging as *gero-transcendence* (Tornstam, 1996). Here, there is a shift in perspective, from a materialistic and rational vision to a cosmic one. Solitude becomes prized and ripe with meaning. We increase our affinity with the present, past, and coming generations. We move beyond a fear of death to an acceptance of its inevitability. As a woman in one of my workshops commented, "I really feel that I've come to the point where I can honestly say that I've lived a very full life; I could go anytime. It would upset my kids to hear me say that, but it's actually a positive feeling for me. I really feel grateful for all of my life."

The life stories I have collected dovetail nicely with the work of Reischer et al. (2021), who suggest that self-transcendent individuals tend to narrate their experiences as spiritual journeys of humanistic growth. Reminiscent of Erikson's idea of integrity, they identified themes of closure (emotional resolution), interconnectedness, lifelong learning, secure attachments, self-actualization, and spiritual pluralism.

Bauer's seminal work detailing the two broad paths of personal development–one of wisdom, which emphasizes values, and one of well-being, which emphasizes happiness – describes that a good life story creates the conditions for these outcomes (Bauer, 2021). The transcendent self-story characterized by growth ultimately moves beyond story and into an arena similar to the experiences described earlier in this paper. It shifts into the phenomenon of experiencing oneself as expanding backward and forward in time, a feeling of connectedness to all of humanity.

The author Dani Shapiro describes this beautifully in her novel *Signal Fires*: "It looks as if the sea were filled with thousands upon thousands of flickering stars. Perhaps each one is what remains of every soul who has ever lived; perhaps time is not a continuum, but rather, past, present, and future are always and forever unspooling" (Shapiro, 2022, pg. 217).

The trip to bountiful

Randall describes aging as a "pulling together of the self" (Randall & McKim, 2008). In my work as a therapist, I'm often struck by how much more difficult it can be for younger adults to put their experience in perspective; older adults seem to have an easier time connecting the dots, stepping back, and making linkages. On woman put it so well:

> I've always love to dance; Joe is a terrible dancer. Over the years I've tried everything: shaming him, dragging him to dance classes, refusing to dance with him. Why, I used to actually say to his face, 'You stink. You have no rhythm. You are hopeless.' Can you

> believe that? Now I wonder how I could be so cruel. These days, I'm grateful that he still wants to dance with me, that he tries, and I don't care how we look when we get on the dance floor at weddings. I realize he asks me because he knows how much it means to me to dance, and for that I'm very grateful.

This is the kind of perspective that can be assisted in a therapeutic process; when it occurs organically, it is an example of the magic and mystery of human development. By late adulthood, we have opportunities to see our stories gain definition. What may have been hovering on the horizon, vaguely outlined and familiar in its basic form, is now called home from its liminal borders to form a shape that carries dimension, heft, and meaning. It can indeed be a time of integrity.

My most recent "near occasion of soul" is an example of this pulling together, again remarkable in the organic, effortless way it came about.

As a longtime advocate of life review and reminiscence (Birren & Cochran, 2001), I had been reflecting on two long-standing regrets, one professional and one personal. I began a deep dive into the literature on regret and remorse. Daniel Pink (2022) conducted a survey in 2020 of more than fifteen thousand people in 105 countries. It asked the question, "How often do you look back on your life and wish you had done things differently?" Of the respondents, roughly 80% had regrets occasionally; 20% said they feel regret "all the time." Pink then categorized the types of regret his respondents reported and sorted them into four types, which he identified as foundation regrets, boldness regrets, moral regrets, and connection regrets. A foundation regret is one in which we regret a choice we made that affected the course of our life. A boldness regret is one in which we did not do something that had long-term consequences for our life and, in hindsight, wish we had taken the chance we rejected. A moral regret comes when we acknowledge that we violated our own standards or values. Some regrets are combinations of types, and it was clear to me that my regrets definitely commingled.

On the professional front, I regret that I did not narrow my focus to academics instead of pursuing multiple directions simultaneously. This has been easier to put into perspective by weighing the imagined gains and losses. The personal regret had to do with a growing realization that in my mid twenties, I had agreed to a relationship I knew I wasn't ready for – a self-betrayal of sorts – particularly since I continued to cling to it out of a misplaced loyalty. This regret bore elements of all types of regret and has been much more challenging to face because making a change would impact other individuals as well as me.

During this review, I became aware of my longing to return to a church community, which I experienced as a kind of spiritual urgency. I had long appreciated the value of community worship, starting in childhood and lasting through adulthood, when I was very active in a local congregational church. During my empty-nest years, that church incurred the loss of a beloved minister, which was followed by a number of other disruptions that gutted its membership. While I sorely missed the sense of belonging, I had felt disconnected from the community, even sad, following each worship experience. Long a believer in being part of the solution, not the problem, I hung on, thinking surely things would turn around. I even held a vision of my celebration-of-life service in the church's sanctuary. There was that loyalty; I again ignored my feelings of dissatisfaction.

After a period of church shopping, I began attending the congregational church in a nearby town. I was overcome by the immediate warmth of welcome and the vital community, which spoke to so many of my interests. I had a powerful sense of a rightness of fit, that I had come home. The opportunities to engage in social justice work, and the richness of spiritual offerings, brought me alive in unexpected ways. After I had been attending for several weeks, they had a new-member orientation, and I impulsively signed up. I am grateful every day that I joined. It was the first time I had challenged my long-held belief – my story theme – that I should be loyal or risk abandonment. Instead, I found a greater freedom and vitality than I had ever imagined possible. In this seemingly miraculous process, I rewrote one of my earliest themes, changing my adoption story from one of fear of abandonment to a grown-up version of belonging and self-efficacy.

Throughout this experience, I again appreciated the wisdom of psychologist Carol Gilligan, who refashioned human development to include the experiences of women. Her seminal work, *In a Different Voice* (Harvard University Press, 1982), recasts the conversation about self and morality to a conversation about voice and relationship. She challenges women to claim their agency (voice) instead of sacrificing it in the name of goodness.

The pinnacle of women's development hinges on our ability to include ourselves as objects of care. I realized that was exactly what I had done in my so-called impulsive decision to leave one church and join another. Surely my outdated self-silencing – abdicating my truest desires and the voice of my deepest integrity and wisdom – was in the throes of change. To return to the work of John O'Donohue:

> There is great difference between knowledge and wisdom. You can know many things, you can know a lot of facts about things, even facts about yourself, but it is the truths that you realize yourself that move deeply into you. Wisdom, then, is a deeper way of knowing. Wisdom is the art of living in rhythm with your soul, your life, and the divine. Wisdom is the way that you learn to decipher the unknown; and the unknown is our closest companion. So wisdom is the art of being courageous and generous with the unknown, of being able to decipher and recognize its treasures (O'Donohue, p.194).

I look forward to having more space to become acquainted with my changing self. That is the gift of aging. This includes expanding my senses, expanding my openness to experience, and looking for the mystery and magic in momentary presence.

What, if anything, I will do with these insights remains to be seen. How will I respond to this inner call to repair (Weingarten, 2023)? Will I end a long-term relationship, fully retire, retire sooner, pepper my speech with more no-thank-yous? For now, I'm engaging in the creative tension of resisting doing and concentrating on being. I am aware of a greater compassion for that early narrator, who felt her very existence depended on being a good carer of others. I think less about the idea that we shed stories as we change and more about the power of various compelling stories that become competitive for primacy at different times. Rewriting my stories is a process of deconstructing my long-standing stories (old notions of self) and reweaving themes and meanings into a fresh tapestry. I am more fully embracing the shift from earning my right to exist to being enough as-is, which helps me to thaw out my heart and to feel and take in the love of others. The shift from living life as the one "given away" to the one who is well chosen and well loved has been profound. Our stories matter because they help set the level of love in our lives.

Perhaps my greater readiness to receive these messages from the soul, without judgment or the need to fix, is the gift of aging. Perhaps these new stories can provide, especially when our nights are dark, a light of hope, a way through.

I am also recasting the storyline of going it alone. Going it alone is (and always was) not only impossible but also blocks awareness of my more sacred longings of the soul and the desire to enter into the vast circle of belonging. I am becoming more inclined to take a hand – many hands, in fact. Now I can see that on my trip to bountiful I have always been accompanied; it is too precious a journey to take alone.

Precious Lord, take my hand
Lead me on, let me stand
I am tired, I'm weak, I am worn
Through the storm, through the night
Lead me on to the light
Take my hand, precious Lord
Lead me home.

Disclosure statement

No potential conflict of interest was reported by the author.

References

Arnett, J. (2015). *Emerging adulthood: The winding road from the late teens through the Twenties* (2nd ed.). Oxford University Press.

Arnett, J., Robinson, O., & Lachman, M. (2020). Rethinking adult development: Introduction to the special issue. *The American Psychologist, 75*(4), 425–431. https://doi.org/10.1037/amp0000633

Aronson, L. (2019). *Elderhood.* Bloomsbury Publishing.

Bauer, J. (2021). *The transcendent self.* Oxford University Press.

Birren, J., & Cochran, K. (2001). *Telling the stories of life through guided autobiography groups.* Johns Hopkins University Press.

Carstensen, L., Issacowitz, D., & Charles, S. (1999). Taking time seriously: A theory of socio-emotional selectivity. *The American Psychologist, 54*(3), 1654–1681. https://doi.org/10.1037/0003-066X.54.3.165

Carstensen, L., Turan, B., Scheibe, S., Ram, N., Ersner-Hershfield, H., Samanez Larkin, G., Brooks, K., & Nesselroade, J. (2011). Emotional experience improves with age: Evidence based on over 10 years of experiential sampling. *Psychology and Aging, 26*(1), 21–33. https://doi.org/10.1037/a0021285

Cohen, G. D. (2005). *The mature mind: The positive power of the aging brain.* Basic Books.

Csikszentmihalyi, M., & Csikszentmihalyi, I. (1988). *Optimal experience: Psychological studies of flow in consciousness.* Cambridge University Press.

Diehl, M., Smyer, M., & Mehrotta, C. (2020). Optimizing aging: A call for a new narrative. *The American Psychologist, 75*(4), 577–589. https://doi.org/10.1037/amp0000598

Elder, G., Johnson, M., & Crosnoe, R. (2003). The emergence and development of life course theory. In J. T. Mortimer & M. J. Shanahan (Eds.), *Handbook of the life course* (pp. 3–19). Handbooks of Sociology and Social Research.

Erikson, E. H. (1968). *Identity: Youth and crisis.* W. W. Norton.

Gilligan, Carol. (1982). In a Different Voice. Harvard University Press, Cambridge, MA.

Gullette, M. (2004). *Aged by culture.* University of Chicago Press.

Hinrichsen, G. (2023). A New concept of aging. *Monitor on Psychology, 3*(23), 38–43.

Levy, B. (2022). *Breaking the age code: How your beliefs about aging determine how long and how well you live.* William Morrow.

Marsh, L., Edginton, T., Conway, M., & Loveday, C. (2019). Positivity bias in past and future episodic thinking: Relationship with anxiety, depression, and retrieval-induced forgetting. *The Quarterly Journal of Experimental Psychology, 7*(3), 508–522. https://doi.org/10.1177/1747021818758620

Mather, M., Jacobsen, L., & Pollard, K. (2015). Aging in the United States. *Population Bulletin, 70*(2–4).

McAdams, D. P. (1995). What do we know when we know a person? *Journal of Personality, 63* (3), 365–396. https://doi.org/10.1111/j.1467-6494.1995.tb00500.x

McAdams, D. P. (2015). *The art and science of personality development.* Guilford Press.

McAdams, D. P., & Cox, K. S. (2010). Self and identity across the life span. In R. M. Lerner, M. E. Lamb, & A. M. Freund (Eds.), *The handbook of life-span development*, New York, NY: Wiley.

McAdams, D. P., & McLean, K. C. (2013). Narrative identity. *Current Directions in Psychological Science, 22*(3). https://doi.org/10.1177/0963721413475622

Neugarten, B. (1972). Personality and the Aging Process. *The Gerontologist, 12*(1), 9–15. https://doi.org/10.1093/geront/12.1_Part_1.9

O'Donohue, J. (1997). *Anam Cara: A Book of Celtic Wisdom.* Cliff Street Books.

Pink, D. (2022). *The power of regret: How looking backward moves us forward.* Riverhead Books.

Randall, W., & Kenyon, G. (2001). *Ordinary Wisdom: Biographical Aging and the Journey of Life.* Praeger.

Randall, W., & McKim, E. (2008). *The poetics of growing old.* Oxford University Press.

Reischer, H., Roth, L., Villarreal, J., & McAdams, D. (2021). Self- transcendence and live stories of humanistic growth among late-midlife adults. *Journal of Personality*, *89*(2), 305–324. https://doi.org/10.1111/jopy.12583

Rohr, R. (2011). *Breathing under water: Spirituality and the twelve steps*. St. Anthony Messenger Press.

Rohr, R. (2013). *Immortal Diamond: The Search for Our True Self*. Wiley & Sons.

Siegel, D. (2016). *Mind: A journey to the heart of being human*. Norton & Co.

Singer, J., & Skerrett, K. (2014). *Positive couple therapy: Using we-stories to enhance resilience*. Routledge Press.

Skerrett, K. (2016). We-ness and the cultivation of wisdom in couple therapy. *Family Process*, *55*(1), 48–61. https://doi.org/10.1111/famp.12162

Skerrett, K. (2022). *Growing married: Creating stories for a lifetime of love*. Lifecycle Press.

Skerrett, K., & Fergus, K. (Eds.). (2015). *Couple Resilience*. Springer Press.

Skerrett, K., Spira, M., & Chandy, J. (2021). Emerging elderhood: Transitions from midlife. *Clinical Social Work Journal*, *50*(4), 377–386. https://doi.org/10.1007/s10615-021-00791-2

Staudinger, U. (2020). The positive plasticity of adult development: Potential for the 21st century. *The American Psychologist*, *75*(4), 540–553. https://doi.org/10.1037/amp0000612

Tornstam, L. (1996). Gerotranscendence: A theory about maturing into old age. *Journal of Aging and Identity*, *1*(1), 37–49.

Weingarten, K. (2023). Called to repair injustice: Connecting everyday practices to societal phenomena, creating momentum for solidarity and change. *Family Process*, *62*(1), 6–34. https://doi.org/10.1111/famp.12839

Zweig, C. (2021). *The inner work of age: Shifting from role to soul*. Park Street Press.

Index

Note: Page numbers followed by "n" denote endnotes.